Conscientious Objection and Human Rights

Conscientious Objection and Human Rights

A Systematic Analysis

By

Grégor Puppinck

BRILL

LEIDEN | BOSTON

Library of Congress Control Number: 2016961562

Typeface for the Latin, Greek, and Cyrillic scripts: "Brill". See and download: brill.com/brill-typeface.

ISBN 978-90-04-34159-3 (paperback)
ISBN 978-90-04-34160-9 (e-book)

Originally published as Volume 1(1) 2017, in *Law and Religion*, DOI 10.1163/24682993-12340001.

This book is printed on acid-free paper and produced in a sustainable manner.

Contents

Conscientious Objection and Human Rights: A Systematic Analysis

Grégor Puppinck, PhD
Director of the *European Centre for Law and Justice*
Member of the Panel of experts of the OSCE/ODIHR on freedom of religion and belief
g.puppinck@gmail.com

Abstract

This study analyses the notion of 'conscientious objection' with the aim of identifying criteria in order to determine to what extent it is legitimate, in view of freedom of conscience and religion, to sanction individuals for refusing to take part in an activity which they claim to be incompatible with their convictions. First the study clarifies concepts of conscientious objection. Then it examines the case law of international bodies and draws distinctions in order to differentiate several types of objection, and from here it identifies evaluation criteria appropriate to the distinctions which emerge in those objection types. Finally, the study proposes what rights and obligations arise for the State as to the different types of objection.

Keywords

Freedom of conscience – freedom of religion – conscientious objection – moral

* The author extends his warmest thanks to Dr Vincent Cador and Dr Claire de la Hougue for their advice and contributions, and to Mr François Thouvenin for having translated this study. A previous version of this study has been published in French in *Société, Droit et Religion*, n° 6, July 2016, CNRS Editions.

 | DOI 10.1163/9789004341593_001

Introduction

> *To what extent is it legitimate under Article 9 of the [European] Convention [for the Protection of Human Rights and Fundamental Freedom, among which freedom of conscience and religion is guaranteed by this Article] to oblige individuals to take part in an activity incompatible with their beliefs?*

This question, raised by Judge Fischback in his dissenting opinion joined to the judgment relating to the case of *Chassagnou and others v. France*[1] on conscientious objection to hunting, is likely to arise in many areas where the convictions of an individual may conflict with the demands of the law or of a superior.

The right to conscientious objection can be seen as a 'legal monster' increasingly called upon under the influence of both the growing pluralism of society and the disconnection between law and morals. As proof of this phenomenon, cases of persons who, in the name of their conscience, refuse to perform military service, to swear on the Bible, to celebrate same-sex unions, to allow hunting on their land, to take part in an abortion, to have their children vaccinated or to let their children attend compulsory classes in ethics, religion or sexual education are constantly referred to the European Court of Human Rights. Moreover, this Court has to judge cases about refusals with regard to blood transfusions, paying taxes, observing a religious activity, or respecting a prohibition to wear religious clothing and signs.

If legislators and judges have to decide on the merits of every objection, it is feared that, overwhelmed by different requests, they will end up rejecting all objections in the name of equality before positive law. This will negate the guarantee of freedom of conscience and religion. It is therefore necessary to clarify the notion of conscientious objection in order not to enlarge its field of application to the point of making it indefensible, but rather to better define it so that it may be guaranteed to an extent that is fair.

The following study seeks to propose such a clarification, and it does so by highlighting the rational aspects of the concept of conscientious objection; this requires avoiding excessive subjectivism or positivism, each of which respectively may afford too much or too little legitimacy to individual conscience. In the course of our reflection on conscientious objection, between positivism and subjectivism we shall endeavour to seek the objectivity of justice—and whether the object of justice resides in actions or in persons.

---

1 ECHR, *Chassagnou and others v. France*, GC, n° 25088/94, 28331/95 and 28443/95, 29 April 1999.

After clarifying concepts associated with conscientious objection, such as conscience, beliefs, objection, *forum internum* and *forum externum* (Part I), this study will identify examples of conscientious objection recognised by positive law, from the point of view of both the duty and the right to object (Part II). From here it identifies evaluation criteria appropriate to the distinctions which emerge in those objection types (Part III). Finally, the study proposes what rights and obligations arise for the State as to the different types of objection (Part IV).

I Conscientious Objection: A Clarification of Concepts

Conscientious objection touches upon different concepts which often have blurred definitions: conscience, belief, objection, *forum internum* and *forum externum*. It is necessary to clarify these categories in order to understand what exactly is meant by conscientious objection.

1 *Conscience*

Conscience is not the whole set of personal beliefs specific to an individual; it is the practical origin of these beliefs, their source.[2] Conscience has a very peculiar psychological and moral function: it delivers, through reason, judgments about the morality of practical situations and is therefore able to judge social and religious norms.

a Psychological and Moral Functions of Conscience

Both the English and German languages have two different words to express what in French is classified under the general term *'conscience'*, in both its psychological and moral aspects. In English and German, psychological conscience is called *consciousness* and *Bewusstein*, respectively, whereas moral conscience is called *conscience* and *Gewissen*, respectively.

i *Psychological Conscience*

Conscience is first an act of knowledge of the world and oneself. It is open to the knowledge of everything universal and particular. Its existence is made possible by the reflecting nature of human intelligence, namely man's ability

2 For instance, the ECtHR, in *Bayatyan v. Armenia*, GC, n° 23459/03, 7 July 2011, does not definitely separate these two notions when it speaks of the conflict between *"the obligation to serve in the army and a person's conscience or his deeply and genuinely held religious or other beliefs"*.

to know that he/she[3] has a knowledge, and hence the ability to possess a self-knowledge. This reflecting look of intelligence through which a person is able to apprehend oneself and to encompass the world spiritually is strictly specific to man. In contrast to animals, man has a mind which opens him to self-knowledge. Such a knowledge is precisely the psychological conscience and can be analysed as a form of lucidity, an 'apperception' in the philosophical meaning of the term: the person is able to enter oneself, to know oneself, to self-apprehend and to distinguish oneself from the world. So the conscience, which can be shared with other persons, bears witness to the existence and doings of the subject (excluding his unconscious activity).

ii *Moral Conscience*

Though moral conscience is effectively rooted in psychological conscience, it goes a step further, since it adds a moral judgment to the latter as far as action is concerned: the person not only knows what he does, but he assesses the morality of his action. The *Grand dictionnaire Robert* defines in this sense the moral conscience as "*the intuitive knowledge by the human being of what is good and evil, and what prompts him to pass judgment on the moral value of his own acts.*"[4] The Catechism of the Catholic Church defines moral conscience as: "*a judgment of reason whereby the human person recognises the moral quality of a concrete act*".[5] For St. Thomas Aquinas, it is '*an application of knowledge to the act*', an act accomplished with knowledge, '*cum scientia*'. For Emmanuel Kant, it is '*the expression of practical reason*', i.e. the means by which every person exercises his reason in practical, concrete situations with a view to do good. Moreover, it is possible to distinguish between the possession of moral sense, called '*habitual conscience*', and its use in every particular circumstance, called '*actual conscience*'.

Moral conscience is moved internally by a desire to do good and, hence, by a rejection of evil. This desire to do good is the deepest source of our actions which are configured to it, the good being then their cause and norm. Everything that contributes to the self-accomplishment of the person is desired as good, and everything that causes harm is rejected as evil. Conscience exercises its judgment

---

3 TN: Needless to say, every mention of "man", "human being", "person", "somebody", "someone", etc. in this text must be understood as referring to any individual belonging to the human species, whatever their sex. But for easier reading, only the masculine will be used henceforth.

4 TN: *« la connaissance intuitive par l'être humain de ce qui est bien et mal, et ce qui le pousse à porter des jugements de valeur morale sur ses propres actes ».*

5 Catechism of the Catholic Church, n° 1778.

in the light of such internal appeal. This judgment is exercised by reason, by intelligence, in so far as the latter seeks to identify in every situation, among the various choices open to us, which of them makes it possible to reach the highest good, and which most conform to the truth.

These fundamental principles of morals—'*doing good and avoiding evil*'—are present in every person; it is the 'habitual conscience', also called '*synderesis*'. So, the perception of these principles of morals recognised as universal is, according to Cicero, an innate law which cannot be lost;[6] and according to Seneca, "*The sacred spirit* [which] *sits in us, an observer and guardian of our acts, good or bad*".[7] This is why the Greeks and Hebrews use the word "heart" to refer to conscience as the source of moral life.

Such basic desire for good for oneself manifests itself in the "golden rule" of reciprocity: "*Never do to anyone else anything that you would not want someone to do to you.*"[8] This golden rule is one of the elementary conditions of social life and can be found in most traditional wisdoms.[9] So, the Hindi translation prescribes this: "*You should not do to anyone else what you consider as harmful for yourself*",[10] whereas Confucius recommends: "*What you would not like to be done to you, do not inflict it upon others*".[11]

b The Mechanism of Moral Conscience

Moral conscience is an act of judgment by the reason, right and enlightened (*iudicium rationis*), which applies the knowledge of moral principles (habitual conscience or synderesis) to a concrete situation. Conscience, being informed by synderesis, thus proceeds by syllogism to the moral evaluation of a concrete situation. It can deal with a past situation as well as with a present or planned action, both with oneself and the external world, for example with an order: its scope is universal.

The right exercise of conscience nevertheless implies that the person is able to form his judgment without undue influence and in the light of information allowing him to judge *cum scientia*, i.e. with knowledge of the facts. Conscience's judgment necessarily derives from a discernment achieved

6 "*Non scripta sed natal ex*", *Pro Milone*, 10.

7 Seneca, *Epistulae ad Lucilium*, 41.2.

8 Book of Tobias, 4, 15.

9 Christianity goes further, since it recommends not only refraining from doing harm, but also positively doing to anyone else what you would want someone to do to you.

10 *Mahābhārata, Anusasana parva*, 1, 13, 3–9 (ed. Ishwar Chundra Sharma and O.N. Bimali; transl. According M.N. Dutt, Parimal Publications, Dehli, vol. IX, p. 469).

11 *Confucius, Entretiens* 15, 23; French translation by A. Cheng, Paris, 1981, p. 125.

through reason, since it consists in applying the principles of morals to any given circumstance, taking into account the whole knowledge available to this conscience. Now, the conscience of a person who is ill-informed (unenlightened) or even manipulated (for instance by sectarian or ideological movements), or under the influence of passion, would be obscured, and this would affect the very freedom of such person. For this reason, everybody is morally responsible not only *before* his conscience, but also *of* his conscience, and therefore he should form it accordingly.

The right exercise of conscience implies, moreover, that the person knows how to reason in a rigorous and earnest way, with a right reason (*recta ratio*). It is therefore self-evident that a person suffering from dementia has no more reliable conscience than a child, all the more so as he could not be held criminally responsible.[12] However, ignorance, affectivity and habits[13] can also affect conscience. In this sense, the training of reason, the critical mind and instruction contribute towards the true freedom of consciences, thereby allowing everyone to form good judgments about the morality of their acts. Conscience operates all the more efficiently since it is enlightened and sustained by right reason.

Moral conscience is therefore not an *arbitrary* act; it is the act of *knowledge* of that which is good; it does not generate a moral obligation, but recognises it (with a risk of error) in the light of the synderesis from which it draws its authority. Consequently, a person is not master of his own conscience (in Victor Hugo's poem *La conscience*, Cain cannot escape the eye of his conscience peering at him even in his very tomb[14]); at the most, he only can try to choke and obscure it. Freedom of conscience is not a moral freedom, meaning nobody can make an arbitrary moral judgment. A person can exercise his free will when he has to choose between following or rejecting what he is ordered by his conscience. The person, equally moved by his affection, can then act against his own conscience: *I know* (*by my conscience*) *that it is wrong to steal this object, but I still choose to do it* (*by my free will*), *since my lust* (*desire*) *is stronger than my moral sense*.[15] In this way, moral conscience commits the person, because it shows the moral evaluation of his planned action to his free will. Therefore, the person will act consciously and will be able to answer for his acts: he will be responsible for them.

---

12 But the ignorant is responsible for the poor training of his conscience.

13 St. Thomas Aquinas defines constraint, ignorance, passion and habit as affecting freedom of decision.

14 *"L'œil était dans la tombe et regardait Caïn."*

15 See for example Romans, 7; 15.

Some individuals can be mistaken, and their conscience can be erroneous; however, this error is but an accident and does not annihilate the general value of conscience, which is basically good and offers a reliable instrument to govern our actions, as witnessed by the countless decisions that conscience enlightens in daily life.

c Social and Religious Norms are Transcended through the Moral Sense Perceived by Personal Conscience

Personal conscience allows everyone to judge whether a planned action aims at a real and desirable good, and whether the means employed to this end are appropriate. If such is the case, the individual can, by his free will, desire this good and implement the means necessary to obtain it. Also, personal conscience allows everyone to judge whether an action recommended by a third person is aimed at a real and desirable good. The individual concerned then makes in conscience a judgment on the different social, legal and religious standards addressed to him before he decides to comply with them or not. In that respect, it can be said that personal conscience transcends social and religious standards, since it does not melt into the latter, and is therefore sufficiently independent of them to pass judgment on them.

A free person does not act like a robot which obeys blindly: he internalizes the orders received and checks whether they are aimed at some good before executing them, if appropriate. The binding nature of any order is due not so much to the formal authority of the one who gave it as to the perception, by the one who received it, of the moral obligation to act for the good to which such order must be adjusted. This moral obligation, proceeding from a personal will to attain the aforementioned good, represents the principle of what drives a man to respect the law. In this way, obedience to different standards is neither direct nor automatic: it passes through the internal examination of personal conscience, then through free will.

Every person judges in conscience the orders and social standards meant for him. By this judgment, the individual recognises that he has a personal moral obligation prevailing over social standards, whether it confirms and endorses them or condemns and rejects them. In an optimal situation, the law aims at justice and common good and enlightens the conscience of individuals who can in turn adjust themselves to this good by obeying the law. Prior to its binding function, the law has an educational function: showing the individual the good to be sought and arousing in him a desire for it, i.e. his involvement, so that he consciously and deliberately applies the social standard and, in so doing, accomplishes the good that he has in common with society. Conversely, a standard deemed in conscience contrary to the real good cannot be desired;

on the contrary, it will be rejected and consequently have no other authority than the strength of the will of the authority which has prescribed it. In others words, such a standard will be received as violence by anyone whose conscience perceives it as an evil.[16] Hence our personal autonomy has its true origin in the transcendence of good as perceived by our personal conscience over any standard.

Thus, everyone exerts critical thinking over different social standards, and this ability is the source of both his moral freedom and his responsibility. That public authorities must respect such "transcendence" is an essential condition for the foundation of a society aimed at seeking what is just, because in so doing, those authorities accept the criticism expressed by individuals. Moreover, they recognise that law cannot be the omega of justice, and that its respect does not result from its formalism, but should be deserved and focused toward good. For a State, therefore, to recognise freedom of conscience *"is to admit that there exists a dimension of man over which it* [*the State*] *has no grip, it is to give up being a totalitarian State"*.[17]

Now, the authorities too often prefer—and even demand—that individuals blindly comply with their directives. Such compliance is required for the sake of a positivist legalism which turns positive law into the omega of justice, this law being then considered as the expression and symbol of a 'collective conscience' that is supposed to overstep and absorb personal consciences. In fact, the assertion that a 'social conscience' exists is the basis of all kinds of totalitarianism, and by smothering personal consciences, such a social conscience stifles the very possibility of free will. Personal moral conscience has its enemies, such as Nietzsche, who accused it of being a '*terrible disease*' perverting the human mind.[18] Hitler, too, wanted to *"free man from a degrading*

16 Does law draw its strength from the intelligence of the individual who complies with it or from the will of the one who is in command? Normally, it does so from both. This question covers the classical distinction between law as *jus* and law as *lex*. In the first acceptation (*jus*), the law is conformed with what is just, while in the second acceptation (*lex*), it is enacted by the authority to guarantee what is just, but can depart from it. If the law-*lex* guarantees the law-*jus*, it draws its strength from the intelligence of the individual who recognises it as good and complies with it. If it does not, then its strength is but the strength of will of the one who is in command, and it constitutes a violance for the individual whose intelligence recognises it as evil.

17 *«... c'est admettre qu'il existe une dimension de l'homme sur laquelle il n'a pas de prise, c'est renoncer à être un État totalitaire »*. Claire de Beausse de la Hougue, *La liberté religieuse en Europe*, ANRT, 2005, p. 9.

18 Friedrich Nietzsche, *Genealogy of Morals*.

chimera called conscience or morals",[19] and one of Nazi slogans stated that "*The Germans' conscience is called Adolf Hitler*".[20] An important institution describes itself today as "*The Conscience of Europe*".[21] Similarly, some religions leave little or no space to personal conscience. According to the dominant Muslim ethics, for instance, "[*O*]*nly the positive revelation of God defines good and evil, just and unjust*", as opposed to personal conscience. Such an ethics is "*fundamentally a morality of obedience. To do good is to obey the commandments; to do evil is to disobey them. Human reason intervenes to recognise the revealed character of the law and to derive from it the concrete juridical implications.*"[22]

When the person lets his individual conscience melt into the party's or religion's conscience, his obedience becomes a blind one. He loses the use of his freedom. Conversely, when a person keeps his critical thinking, he must then—through his free will—decide upon his attitude towards an order which society purports to impose on him and which his conscience reproves. His moral responsibility is entirely committed by such a choice, which can be conscientious objection.

2 *Convictions (or Beliefs)*

'Convictions' are not to be confused with conscience, since they are the judgments passed by it, or the 'reasoned certainties' (according to the *Littré* dictionary[23]) to which the conscience's activity leads: the person is convinced of the truth of his conclusions at the end of a discernment, the quality of which depends on his reason's light and rightfulness. To have a conviction is to be convinced, to be 'vanquished',[24] by a certainty which imposes itself on our intelligence, i.e. by the truth of a particular good. So our judgment is the act by which we recognise ourselves as convinced (or 'vanquished'). Then, convictions are not arbitrary or fancy opinions; they express an inner imperative. The

19 Hermann Rauschning, *Hitler m'a dit, Conférences du Führer sur son plan de conquête du monde*, Paris, 1939. Cited by Jean-Pascal Perrenx, *Théologie morale fondamentale. Tome 3: La conscience*, Ed. Tequi, 2008, p. 42.

20 André Duvignau, « La conscience », *Le bon combat*, 298.072 (2006) 4.

21 The dissenting judges in *Lambert and others v. France*, GC, n° 46043/14, 5 June 2015, strongly criticized the European Court of Human Rights for having attributed to itself this title.

22 International Theological Commission, *In Search of a Universal Ethics: A New Look at the Natural Law*, 2009.

23 *Certitudes raisonnées*: one of the definitions of belief by the *Littré*.

24 TN: Untranslatable wordplay over "convaincu" and "vaincu", from the same Latin origin. To be "convinced" and to be "vinced".

"prescriptions of conscience" are convictions about what should or should not be done.

Therefore, conscience is not free as to the object of what it is looking for: the individual resists, doubts, defends himself, asks himself about the truth of good and evil until he 'surrenders to evidence', to the belief which imposes itself on him. Scientific research is based on the fact that conscience is held by reason and dependent on the quality of information upon which it can judge. Like any scientist, a sincere man is not free to choose the beliefs he is led to; at most, he can reconsider them. Sciences, including moral sciences (and Law is included among them) are based on the objectivity of conscience, though judgments can be affected by errors tainting the reasoning process or the knowledge.

Conscience passes its judgments not only in the innate light of synderesis, but also in the light of acquired knowledge, whether the latter is of a philosophical, religious or factual nature. Then it is possible to distinguish between 'moral convictions', when they derive from the application of synderesis and factual data, and 'religious convictions', when they derive from the application of religious beliefs.

Convictions are not the only expressions of conscience: conscience can remain uncertain and limit itself to *opt* for a judgment it deems probably true; it then has an opinion. Conscience can even remain in doubt; the person then suspends his judgment. Opinion and doubt are not convictions. Finally, a person may have lost the use of reason (under the influence of passion or disease) or may have never acquired it (as may be the case with a child): in this case too, his judgments are not worthy of being referred to as convictions.

The distinction between conviction and belief is more pronounced in French than in English. Belief would be translated in French by '*croyance*' which is the result of an act of faith (to believe) or of a mere opinion, whereas conviction is deeper and stronger, and the result of reasoning, of reason. We see a difference of nature between convictions and beliefs, convictions being more rational; this is why we will often speak about 'religious beliefs' and 'moral convictions'. This distinction reflects the fundamental differences between faith and reason, between freedom of religion and freedom of conscience.

3 Forum Internum *and* Forum Externum

The classical distinction between *forum internum* and *forum externum* should be explained too, since it helps in understanding the nature and scope of conscientious objection. From here on, we shall deal not only with freedom of conscience, but also with freedom of thought and religion.

Article 9 of the European Convention for the Protection of Human Rights and Fundamental Freedoms (hereinafter "ECHR" or "Convention") guarantees, as a single freedom, *"freedom of thought, conscience and religion"*. Insofar as this freedom implies discernment and adhesion to convictions, it primarily concerns the *forum internum*. However, it concerns the *forum externum* too, since it also implies freedom to manifest one's convictions, whether individually and privately, or collectively, in public and within the circle of those with whom one shares the same faith or convictions.[25]

a Forum Internum

Forum internum is the intimate process leading somebody to adopt a conviction; strictly speaking, it is the object of freedom of conscience. As to freedom of conscience *stricto sensu*, it protects the freedom of the process leading somebody to form his conviction. Such process, operated mainly in thought, is internal to the individual. It is, by itself, out of reach of any external constraint (excluding any case of mental manipulation) and must enjoy absolute protection.

Respect for this first aspect of freedom of conscience forbids a person to be forced to adopt a particular belief, hence also to change or not to change his convictions. Moreover, it protects the individual against prosecution motivated only by the content of his convictions—that is to say against "crimes of opinion"; such protection is then constitutive of freedom of thought. In this regard, Article 8, paragraph 2 of the United Nations International Covenant on Civil and Political Rights of 1966 (hereinafter "the Covenant") states that *"No one shall be subject to coercion which would impair his freedom to have or to adopt a religion or belief of his choice."* As to the European Convention on Human Rights, it guarantees in an absolute way *"freedom to change his religion or belief"* and allows restrictions only on *"freedom to manifest one's religion or beliefs"* (Article 9, paragraph 2), not on *"freedom of thought, conscience and religion"* in itself. It is to be noted that the *manifestation* of beliefs covers the freedom of thought and conscience insofar as it manifests itself by the expression of beliefs. The European Court of Human Rights (hereinafter "the European Court" or the ECtHR) and the United Nations Human Rights Committee (hereinafter "the Human Rights Committee") also guarantee in this respect the right of an individual not to *"be compelled to reveal his thoughts or adherence to a religion or belief"*.[26]

---

25 *Bayatyan v. Armenia*, GC, §§ 118 and 119.

26 General Comment 22, Article 18 (Forty-eighth session, 1993). Compilation of General Comments and General Recommendations Adopted by Human Rights Treaty Bodies, U.N. Doc. HRI/GEN/1/Rev.1 at 35 (1994).

b Forum Externum

When a person outwardly manifests his conviction, this manifestation is effected in the *forum externum*. Article 9, paragraph 1 of the Convention stipulates that such manifestation may be carried out *"either alone or in community with others and in public or private* (...), *in worship, teaching, practice and observance".* An almost identical formulation is found in Article 18, paragraph 1 of the Covenant: everyone may manifest his religion or belief *"either individually or in community with others and in public or private,* (...) *in worship, observance, practice and teaching."*

Now, in so far as the *forum externum* is of material nature and part of social life (the *forum*), a manifestation of beliefs within the latter may be subject to restrictions, provided however—as provided by Article 9, paragraph 2 of the Convention—that these are *"prescribed by law"* and *"are necessary in a democratic society in the interests of public safety, for the protection of public order, health or morals, or for the protection of the rights and freedoms of others."*[27]

In summary, the *forum internum* pertains to the being of a person, and the *forum externum* to the actions of a person.

4 *Objection*

"Faced with somebody who pushes us to [do] *what is judged evil by our intelligence, our conscience stands up in the very name of the truth of good, which is the basis of moral obligation";*[28] and deters us from doing such an action. A person's conscience opposes the order as evil, interposes between this order and its accomplishment, and objects to it by anticipation so as to impede it.[29]

While the faculty to adopt convictions and to express them positively is the affirmative mode of freedom of conscience, conscientious objection is the defensive mode of the same freedom: through conscientious objection, the individual defends his freedom to comply with the judgement of his conscience, i.e. with his conviction requiring him not to accomplish a particular action that he judges evil. Therefore, conscientious objection, which specifically concerns the

---

27 Article 18, paragraph 3 of the Covenant of civil and political rights (1966) uses approximately the same terms: *"Freedom to manifest one's religion or beliefs may be subject only to such limitations as are prescribed by law and are necessary to protect public safety, order, health, or morals or the fundamental rights and freedoms of others."*

28 *« Face à celui qui nous engage à* [faire] *ce que notre intelligence juge mauvais, notre conscience se dresse au nom même de la vérité du bien, fondement de l'obligation morale. »* Pascal Jakob, « Objection de conscience », in *Quand le mal devient légal, Objection de la conscience*, L'Homme Nouveau, Hors-série, pp. 21 and 22.

29 "To object" derives from the Latin *ob* and *jacere*, literally, to throw forward.

case where a person refuses to perform a positive and prescribed action, is distinguished from the case where an individual refuses to perform a prohibited action because of his conscience, the latter situation having to do with freedom to manifest positively one's beliefs. Such specificity of objection, as a refusal to act positively, is based moreover on the difference between being forced to act against one's beliefs and being prevented from acting in conformity with them (this point is elaborated on *infra*, in part III).

This faculty to refuse doing an action prescribed by a (social or religious) norm expresses the faculty that every person's conscience possesses to transcend and judge any standard, whether social or religious. Even more so, when an individual willing to obey his conscience accepts in advance a burden imposed by society, he bears witness to the irreducible nature of moral conscience and, hence, to the sense of justice and good, of which this conscience is the ultimate witness and guarantee. The rightfulness of his objection is then worthy of being closely examined by society. Whatever the case, the objector's moral attitude deserves respect.

II Conscientious Objection in Positive Law

Conscientious objection is a component of freedom of conscience, which is itself largely recognised in positive law, especially by Articles 18 of the Covenant and 9 of the European Convention. More fundamentally, the right to freedom of conscience is based directly on Article 1 of the Universal Declaration of Human Rights, which states that all human beings "*... are endowed with reason and conscience and should act towards one another in a spirit of brotherhood*". Reason and conscience are a condition of morality, justice and responsibility. Man's dignity lies, *inter alia*, in the fact of not being driven only by instincts (unlike animals) and acting with altruism. As Heiner Bielefeldt, the UN Special Rapporteur on freedom of religion and belief puts it, *"What is at stake in freedom of conscience is no less than the nucleus of moral agency among human beings".*[30] The Final Act of the Helsinki Conference (1975) goes further by expressly incorporating the right of a person to act *"in accordance with the dictates of his own conscience".*[31]

---

30 Heiner Bielefedt, Nazila Ghanea, Michael Wiener, *Freedom of Religion or Belief, An International Law Commentary*, Oxford University Press, 2016, p. 294.

31 The Final Act stipulates that *"The participating States will respect human rights and fundamental freedoms, including the freedom of thought, conscience, religion or belief, for all* [...] *Within this framework the participating States will recognise and respect the freedom*

Conscience is subject to rights only in so far as it imposes duties on the person. This double aspect appears most clearly in the scheme of conscientious objection, the latter having first to be apprehended as a 'duty' before being possibly recognised as a 'right'.

1 *Conscientious Objection as a Duty*

a In International and European Law

In the aftermath of World War II, and again after the fall of communism, conscientious objection was recognised by contemporary international and European Law as a duty imposing itself on the persons ordered to participate in serious injustices.

The Allied military tribunal at Nuremberg, whose function was to determine the case against war criminals, decided that individuals guilty of crimes against humanity could not be exonerated from their responsibility on account of the fact that they had acted under orders, in the respect of German law. Particularly in the case of the *'Einsatzgruppen'* trial,[32] this tribunal declared that *"The obedience of a soldier is not the obedience of an automaton. A soldier is a reasoning agent. He does not respond, and is not expected to respond, like a piece of machinery."* Faced with a seriously unjust order, the subordinate must refuse to obey: conscientious objection is for him a duty, assuredly a heroic one, but a duty towards humankind (to which he belongs), and the non-respect of which justifies his condemnation. The International Law Commission[33] expressed this principle in the following terms: *"The fact that a person acted pursuant to [an] order of his Government and of a superior does not relieve him from responsibility under international law, provided a moral choice was in fact possible to him."*[34] This possibility of "moral choice" is precisely the faculty exercised by conscience.

---

of the individual to profess and practice, alone or in community with others, religion or belief acting in accordance with the dictates of his own conscience."

32 *United States v. Ohlendorf, and others* ("Einsatzgruppen Trial"), (1948) 4 LRTWC. 470. See Geneviève Dufour, « La défense d'ordres supérieurs existe-t-elle vraiment ? », in *Revue internationale de la Croix-Rouge*, 2000, n° 840.

33 The Charter of the International Military tribunal at Nuremberg, commonly referred to as Charter of Nuremberg, stated: *"The fact that the Defendant acted pursuant to [an] order of his Government or of a superior shall not free him from responsibility, but may be considered in mitigation of punishment if the Tribunal determines that justice so requires."* Agreement for the Prosecution and Punishment of the Major War Criminals of the European Axis. UNTS, vol. 82, p. 279, art. 8.

34 International Law Commission Yearbook, 1950, vol. II, pp. 374–378.

Thus, the non-recognition of a right to conscientious objection by the Nazi regime did not exempt the agents of this regime from their moral and penal obligation of conscientious objection. Their conscience was bound to control, if not the legality of the order received (in relation to the positive "law"), at least—morally—the legitimacy of the order in relation to "the good that should be done and the evil that should be avoided", i.e. to the universal moral order corresponding to fundamental supra-legal standards. It was by referring to the natural right which pre-existed any positive legislation that one could overcome the obstacle due to a formal respect of positive law and condemn the legal positivism addressed at Nuremberg. Besides, it was on the basis of natural law that the contemporary corpus of human rights was re-founded after World War II. The Universal Declaration of Human Rights states in its Preamble that there had been *"barbarous acts which have outraged the conscience of mankind"*. This 'conscience of mankind' is nothing but a universally shared moral sense by which any man should be able to judge the morality of all acts.

After the fall of European communist regimes, the ECtHR, too, was stimulated to recognise the existence of a duty of conscientious objection. It did so especially in *Polednová v. Czech Republic*.[35] This case concerned the participation of a prosecutor, Mrs Polednová, in a political trial held in 1950 in which a Czechoslovakian woman who was a socialist Member of Parliament was sentenced to death for high treason. The Court could not accept *"the applicant's argument according to which she had only obeyed her superiors' instructions"*, since *"she should have been aware of the fact that questions of guilt and penalty had been decided by the political authorities long before the trial and that the fundamental principles of justice were therefore entirely infringed"*.[36] According to the Court, the applicant *"should have been aware;"* she had a duty, as a human with reason and conscience, to exercise her moral judgment and object to the order. It was the breach of this assuredly heroic duty which justified her condemnation. Again, in *K.-H. W. v. Germany*,[37] the Court recognised the legitimacy of the condemnation, by the jurisdictions of reunited Germany, of a border guard of the former Democratic Republic of Germany accused of

35 ECHR, *Polednová v. Czech Republic*, n° 2615/10, 21 June 2011. This case was about the condemnation of a woman charged with taking part, as prosecutor, in a mock trial which led to the pronouncement of a death sentence against four opponents to the Czechoslovakian communist regime.

36 This is a translation, the decision being available only in French.

37 ECHR, *K.-H. W. v. Germany*, GC, n° 37201/97, 22 March 2001. This case concerned a soldier of East Germany who had executed the order to shoot a fugitive at the border.

committing unjust acts. It considered that the soldier *"should have known, as an ordinary citizen, that firing on unarmed persons who were merely trying to leave their country infringed fundamental and human rights"* (§ 104).

Like the Nazi agents at Nuremberg, Mrs Polednová and Mr K.-H. W. were condemned for having complied with orders of public authorities rather than with the prescription to refrain from such compliance that their personal conscience should have given them. Those are real situations where conscientious objection comes into the picture and constitutes a moral, even a legal duty beyond and despite the absence, within the domestic legal order, of a positive right to objection. It is even probable that Mrs Polednová and K.-H. W. would have been condemned by their own national jurisdictions if they had objected to the orders given them. Respect for justice such as it is perceived by conscience sometimes has to be paid at a heroic price. But it is personal conscience, being the ultimate witness to justice, which in the end relates the person and the whole legal order to justice.

b In Domestic Law

The duty of conscientious objection is similarly provided for in domestic law, under certain conditions. In France, for instance, the legislation relating to the civil service recognises the *right* of a civil servant to disobey an order which, though originating from a legitimate authority, is obviously illegal and, above all, likely to compromise a public interest.[38] But the same civil servant is even subject—as is any other person—to a certain *duty* of disobedience in order to avoid being held criminally responsible for the performance of an obviously illegal act.[39] In Germany, the jurisdictions consider that *"the duty of any member of the armed forces to conscientiously execute orders* [...] *does not demand unconditional obedience, but implies a well-considered obedience, especially as to the consequences of the execution of an order, taking into account the limits imposed by the law in force and the ethical points of reference of his own conscience."*[40] Here again, human conscience is the ultimate safeguard.

Concerning professions regulated by a deontology, this duty is expressly provided for. The members of these professions must exercise their profession with conscience. Preservation of the freedom of conscience of lawyers and

---

38 Article 28 of Title I of the French General Statute of civil servants (*Statut général des fonctionnaires*) specifies that a civil servant does not have to obey if *"the order given is obviously illegal and likely to seriously compromise a public interest".*

39 See Article 122–4 of the French penal code.

40 Administrative Tribunal of Germany, 21 June 2005, cited and translated in French by C. Vigouroux, *Déontologie des fonctions publiques*, Dalloz, 2006, coll. "Praxis", p. 377.

physicians against undue pressure requires that they cannot be subject to an external hierarchical power. Moreover, it is because a physician has the duty to exercise his profession *"with conscience and dignity"*[41] that his *"duty to refuse his care for professional or personal reasons"*,[42] *"except in case of emergency or if doing so, he would fail in his duty of humanity"* is recognised.

So, before it can become a 'right', conscientious objection is first and foremost a moral and legal 'duty' which forces a person or a group of persons to reject executing an unjust order. However, beside the *duty* of objection, a *right* to conscientious objection has gradually been recognised so that objectors may follow the prescriptions of their conscience without having to lose their job, their freedom or their life.

2 *Conscientious Objection as a Right*

Conscientious objection is also a right. In so far as duties and rights are correlated and cause each other, the recognition of a duty of objection theoretically implies the recognition of a corresponding right. The recognition of a right to conscientious objection does not raise any theoretical problem in international and European law, since the latter recognises this right as a way of exercising freedom of conscience, which it guarantees especially to individuals against domestic legal orders. In contrast, the recognition of conscientious objection as a right in the domestic order does raise a problem, since it implies an inner contradiction: the same (domestic) legal order sets an obligation, and at the same time, provides for the possibility of not meeting it.

International and European law, as well as positive domestic laws, offer several examples of the recognition of this right. Such examples generally concern matters which have a controversial moral nature or interfere with (religious) prescriptions related to a given cult. Without trying to be comprehensive, we will briefly discuss military service, abortion, euthanasia, hunting, celebration of homosexual unions, taking oaths and religious teaching.

a Refusal of Military Service

It was not until 2006 that the United Nations Human Rights Committee formally recognised the right to conscientious objection to military service under the International Covenant on Civil and Political Rights,[43] but it had "prepared" such recognition beforehand by gradually granting this right an increasingly solid basis. So, by a decision rendered on 7th November 1991 in *J.P. v. Canada*,

---

41 The World Medical Association, *Declaration of Geneva*.

42 Article 47 of the French code of medical deontology in force.

43 See CDH, *L.T.K. v. Finland*, Communication n° 185/1984, dec. 9 July 1985.

it modified its position for the first time and incidentally admitted that *"article 18 of the Covenant certainly protects the right to hold, express and disseminate opinions and beliefs, including conscientious objection to military activities and expenditures"*.[44] Shortly after, in 1993, in its general comment n° 22 on freedom of thought, conscience and religion (Art. 18),[45] while recognising *"that the Covenant does not explicitly refer to a right of conscientious objection"*, the Committee considered for the first time that *"such a right can be derived from article 18, inasmuch as the obligation to use lethal force may seriously conflict with the freedom of conscience and the right to manifest one's religion or belief"* (§ 11). The chairman of the working group, Mr Dimitrijevic, having written this general comment, stated that the conscientious objection referred to *"was not an objection to military service as such but an objection to killing other human beings"*.[46]

In 2006, in *Yeo-Bum Yoon and Myung-Jin Choi v. Republic of Korea*, the Human Rights Committee considered that States which do not admit conscientious objection to the military service contravene Article 18, paragraph 3 of the Covenant. The Committee *"observes that while the right to manifest one's religion or belief does not as such imply the right to refuse all obligations imposed by law, it provides certain protection, consistent with article 18, paragraph 3, against being forced to act against genuinely-held religious belief"* (§ 8.3). It is interesting to note that in this decision, the Committee underlined that conscientious objection to military service represented, in this case, a manifestation of the objectors' belief, that the sanction invoked against them was a restriction by the State of their freedom to manifest their beliefs, and consequently, that such a restriction was admissible only if it was *"prescribed by law and [was] necessary to protect public safety, order, health or morals or the fundamental rights and freedoms of others"* according to Article 18, paragraph 3 of the Covenant. Moreover, the Committee underlined that this restriction *"must not impair the very essence of the right in question"*.[47] The legitimacy of restricting the right to conscientious objection was analysed as if the objection were a manifestation of freedom of conscience. By contrast, a member of the Committee (Mr Solari-Yrigoyen) stated in a separate opinion that the Committee's position should have been based on Article 18, paragraph 1 of the Covenant rather than on

44 HRC, *J.P. v. Canada*, Communication n° 446/1991, 7 November 1991.

45 General comment n° 22 on freedom of thought, conscience and religion, see *supra*.

46 CCPR/C/SR, 1237, § 45.

47 HRC, *Yoon and Choi v. Republic of Korea*, Communication n° 1321–1322/2004, Observations of 3 November 2006; *Jung and others v. Republic of Korea*, Communications n° 1593 to 1603/2007, Observations of 23 March 2010.

Article 18, paragraph 3. If the right to object is based on Article 18, paragraph 1, it then directly guarantees belief and hence cannot be restricted.

By two observations issued in the case of *Jeong and others v. Republic of Korea*[48] (2011), the Human Rights Committee adopted Mr Solari-Yrigoyen's position, and from then on, the right to conscientious objection to military service has been understood as derived directly from the right to freedom of conscience and religion: *"The right of conscientious objection to military service inheres in the right to freedom of thought, conscience and religion. It entitles any individual to an exemption from compulsory military service if this cannot be reconciled with that individual's religion or beliefs. The right must not be impaired by coercion."* (§ 10.4). So this right is deemed by the Committee to form part of the right to freedom of thought, conscience and religion; it is not optional and is not granted by the State. It is implicitly, but necessarily included in freedom of conscience.[49] The Committee added this: *"Repression of the refusal to be drafted for compulsory military service, exercised against persons whose conscience or religion prohibit the use of arms, is incompatible with article 18, paragraph 1, of the Covenant."*[50] This is a meaningful change, since according to the Committee's General observations: *"Article 18 distinguishes the freedom of thought, conscience, religion or belief from the freedom to manifest religion or belief. It does not permit any limitations whatsoever on the freedom of thought and conscience or on the freedom to have or adopt a religion or belief of one's choice"* as guaranteed by Article 18 § 1 of the Covenant.

The Human Rights Committee adopted the same opinion later on, as witnessed in *Atasoy and Sarkut v. Turkey*.[51] Recalling, as it had already said in *Jeong and others v. Republic of Korea*, that the right to conscientious objection to military service *"inheres"* in freedom of conscience—i.e. that it exclusively belongs to the *forum internum*—(in contrast to external manifestations of beliefs in the *forum externum*), the Committee considers that there is no more need to examine the necessity of the punishment (which would be the case if the right to conscientious objection to military service was still based on Article 18, paragraph 3 of the Covenant), but only the effectiveness of this right. Being considered as an element of the *forum internum*, the right to conscientious

48 HRC, *Jeong and others v. Republic of Korea*, Communications n° 1642 to 1741/2007, Observations of 24 March 2011.

49 From *Jeong and others v. Republic of Korea*, 24 March 2011.

50 HRC, *Jong-nam Kim and others v. Republic of Korea*, Communication n° 1786/2008, Observations of 25 October 2012.

51 HRC, *Cenk Atasoy and Arda Sarkut v. Turkey*, Communications n° 1853/2008 and 1854/2008, Observations of 29 March 2012.

objection to military service cannot be restricted, even in the event of exceptional public danger threatening the very existence of the nation (Art. 4.2 of the Covenant). This right to conscientious objection is not a right to perform an alternative service, but indeed a right not to be punished on account of one's refusal. According to the Committee, the State *"may, if it wishes, compel the objector to undertake a civilian alternative to military service, outside of the military sphere and not under military command"*. The State is not obliged to propose an alternative service, but if it so decides, such service must be sufficiently separated from the army and should not be of a punitive nature: it *"must rather be a real service to the community and compatible with respect for human rights"*.[52] The conscientious objector should not be submitted to any punishment.

If this new approach allows asserting the existence of a universal right to conscientious objection to military service, it has significant theoretical implications. Furthemore, several members of the Human Rights Committee have noted an *"important" "error in the analysis"*: considering that *"Refusal to perform military service for reasons of conscience is among the "broad range of acts" encompassed by the freedom to manifest religion or belief in worship, observance, practice and teaching"* and that *"the Committee has not yet provided an adequate justification for its new approach to this issue"*. They have expressed the wish that the latter return to its *"earlier approach, based on the freedom to manifest a religion or belief in practice"*.[53] In their view, refusing to perform military service, like being prevented to wear the Islamic veil, would both imply *manifestations* of beliefs and should be submitted to the same regime.

Other members of the Human Rights Committee (Sir Nigel Rodley, Mr Krister Thelin and Mr Cornelis Flinterman), though sustaining the new approach, have recognised the difficulty to define, within this approach, a criterion about *"how to distinguish conscientious objection to military service from similar objection to paying taxes or, for that matter, compliance with other legal obligations on conscientious grounds."*[54] Indeed, sustaining that the right to conscientious objection to military service is inherent to the right to freedom of thought, conscience and religion raises real questions, such as this one:

---

52 HRC, *Cenk Atasoy and Arda Sarkut v. Turkey*, § 10.4; see also HRC, *Jeong and others v. Republic of Korea*, 24 March 2011.

53 See, in *Cenk Atasoy and Arda Sarkut v. Turkey*, the concurring individual opinion of Mr Gerald L. Neuman, with which Mr Yuji Iwasawa, Mr Michael O'Flaherty and Mr Walter Kaelin associated themselves.

54 Concurring individual opinion of Sir Nigel Rodley, Mr Krister Thelin and Mr Cornelis Flinterman in the HRC case, *Cenk Atasoy and Arda Sarkut v. Turkey*.

what makes conscientious objection to military service inherent to freedom of conscience? Is it *conscientious objection* or *military service*? In other words, is conscientious objection in itself a right inherent to freedom of conscience, or is it the object of objection (in this case military service) which makes the right to objection inherent to the principal right? In fact, it is a question of deciding whether conscientious objection is a *subjective* (*abstract*) *right* asserted by its subject or an *objective* (*concrete*) *right* defined by its object.

It is to be noted that the successive special rapporteurs of the United Nations on freedom of religion or belief have also held either position.[55]

Claiming that the right to conscientious objection is a right in itself (subjective), inherent to freedom of thought, conscience and religion, raises too the question of its necessary concrete limitation, or else this right would be destructive for the legal and moral order. In contrast, claiming that such a right derives from its object implies a judgment about this same object. Though the majority of the Committee has defended the first thesis, several members (led by Sir Nigel Rodley) have underlined that it is because "*the value underlying that right—the sanctity of human life—puts it on another plane than that of other deep human goods protected by the Covenant*". They continued, pointing out: "*Paragraphs 1 and 2 of article 18 acknowledge that completely; paragraph 3 cannot but acknowledge it incompletely. The right to refuse to kill must be accepted completely. That is why article 18, paragraph 3, is the less appropriate basis for the Committee's decision*".[56] So, according to this approach, military service is not the accidental object of objection, it is the very cause of it, it determines it: the right to object does not originate in individual conscience separately, but in the moral problem objectively raised by the fact of killing, namely in its object as apprehended by moral conscience. It is because objection in face of a potential obligation to kill is considered as just in itself, due to its very object, that it benefits everyone, without "*differentiation among conscientious objectors on the basis of the nature of their particular beliefs*".[57] When the objection is deemed justified, the moral or religious nature of the objector's belief is not very relevant: the objection is then justified by its object. On the contrary, when acts are not considered *in se* as justifying an objection, the latter is then apprehended from the subjective point of view.

55 *Heiner* Bielefeldt, and others, *Freedom of Religion or Belief, An International Law Commentary*, p. 269 and following.

56 Concurring individual opinion of Sir Nigel Rodley, Mr Krister Thelin and Mr Cornelis Flinterman in the HRC case, *Cenk Atasoy and Arda Sarkut v. Turkey*.

57 General Comment n° 22, § 11.

We should add it seems that apart from conscientious objection to military service, no case of objection in any other field has been brought before the Human Rights Committee to date. Nevertheless, the HCR has stated, in its decision *Yoon and Choi* of 3 November 2006, that *"while the right to manifest one's religion or belief does not as such imply the right to refuse all obligations imposed by law, it provides certain protection, consistent with article 18, paragraph 3, against being forced to act against genuinely-held religious belief".* This is in effect a protection of a general, if not absolute, right to conscientious objection. At the time of the adoption of this decision, the Human Rights Committee was still analysing conscientious objection as a *manifestation* of freedom of conscience (*forum externum*), susceptible to the limitations provided for in Article 18, paragraph 3 of the Covenant. Its recent case law, which does not admit such a limitation of this right as far as military service is concerned, reinforces the effectivieness of the aforementioned protection, at least against the other practices liable to affect human lives.[58] Logically, and even more so, the Committee should also admit conscientious objection to euthanasia or to abortion, which systematically puts an end to a human life, whereas military service implies only the risk of killing, in the general interest, most often in a situation of need or self-defence and in respect of the law of war.

The development of the European Court of Human Rights' case law offers another example of the great difficulty—which faced the Human Rights Committee—to apprehend the nature and scope of the distinction and logical connection between freedom of conscience and freedom of manifestation, between positive manifestation of beliefs and negative manifestation of them.

So, in 2011, the ECtHR, adopting a dynamic and evolutionary approach to the interpretation of the European Convention, recognised a right to conscientious objection to military service in *Bayatyan v. Armenia.*[59] The Court judged that *"opposition to military service, where it is motivated by a serious and insurmountable conflict between the obligation to serve in the army and a person's conscience or his deeply and genuinely held religious or other beliefs, constitutes a conviction or belief of sufficient cogency, seriousness, cohesion and importance to attract the guarantees of Article 9"* (§ 110). The Court then considered that the refusal to report for military conscription was a "manifestation" of the person's religious beliefs and that the condemnation of the said person for having avoided these military obligations should be analysed as *"an interference with his freedom to manifest his religion as guaranteed by Article 9 § 1"* (§ 112). The

58 According to General Comment n° 22.

59 ECHR, *Bayatyan v. Armenia*, GC.

Court concluded on the violation of Article 9, while underlying that there were effective alternatives likely to spare the competing interests involved.

By adopting such a position in *Bayatyan v. Armenia*, the Court therefore aligned itself with what was then the official position of the United Nations Human Rights Committee, as defined in *Jeong and others v. Republic of Korea*, since it considered that conscientious objection is a manifestation of freedom of conscience and religion, liable to limitation, and that any interference with this right should be justified in view of criteria defined in Article 9, paragraph 2 of the Convention.

While recognising that Article 9 of the Convention contains a right to conscientious objection, the Court also went along with the position defended since 1967 by the Parliamentary Assembly of the Council of Europe (PACE)[60] which recalled, *inter alia*, in a resolution of 2001: *"The right of conscientious objection is a fundamental aspect of the right to freedom of thought, conscience and religion enshrined in the Universal Declaration of Human Rights and the European Convention on Human Rights."*[61] The Court holds the same position as the Committee of Ministers of the Council of Europe[62] and almost all member States of this organisation, since on the day of the judgment, only two States did not recognise conscientious objection to military service.[63]

As for the European Union, it has taken note of this development by integrating the right to conscientious objection into Article 10, paragraph 2 of its Charter of Fundamental Rights. It should be observed that this provision is written in general terms: *"The right to conscientious objection is recognised, in*

60 PACE, Resolution 337 (1967) *on the right of conscientious objection*. See also, *inter alia*, the Recommendation 1518 (2001) of the 1 March 2002, *on the exercise of the right of conscientious objection to military service in Council of Europe member states*, in which the PACE declares that the right to conscientious objection is *"is a fundamental aspect of the right to freedom of thought, conscience and religion"* recognised in the Convention.

61 APCE, Recommendation 1518 (2001), § 8.

62 Committee of Ministers of the Council of Europe, Recommendation R(87)8 of 9 April 1987 *regarding conscientious objection to compulsory military service*, and Recommendation CM/Rec(2010)4 of 24 February 2010 of the Committee of Ministers to member States on the human rights of the members of the armed forces.

63 In *Enver Aydemir v. Turkey* (n° 26012/11) of the 7 May 2016, the Court found that the applicant's objection to performing compulsory military service did not fall within the scope of Article 9 of the Convention because he had not categorically refused to perform compulsory military service, but would be able to do so under a system based on the Koran and subject to its rules. See Frank Cranmer, "Conscientious objection to military service again: *Enver Aydemir v Turkey*" in *Law & Religion UK*, 8 June 2016.

accordance with the national laws governing the exercise of this right"; the provision does not limit conscientious objection to military service.

b Refusal of Abortion and of Certain Biotechnologies

As far as abortion is concerned, the European Court of Human Rights was incidentally driven to state its position in several cases involving Poland. Considering that conscientious objection and access to abortion, which come within the remit of Article 9 (freedom of thought, conscience and religion) and Article 8 (right to respect for one's private and family life) of the Convention respectively, are—in these cases—in conflict one with another, the Court judged that *"States are obliged to organise the health services system in such a way as to ensure that an effective exercise of the freedom of conscience of health professionals in the professional context does not prevent patients from obtaining access to services to which they are entitled under the applicable legislation."*[64] The ECtHR considers as established that health professionals' freedom of conscience manifested by the refusal to perform an abortion should be effectively exercisable.

Most European countries recognise such a right to conscientious objection, implicitly or explicitly, as a 'conscience clause' incorporated in national legislation. So, in France, Article L. 2212–2 of the French Code of public health states, in its first paragraph, that *"[A] doctor is never obliged to perform a voluntary interruption of pregnancy"* and, in its second paragraph, that "[*N*]*o midwife, no male or female nurse, no paramedic, whoever he/she is, is obliged to participate in an interruption of pregnancy."* It can be noted that such conscience clauses constitute the explicit implementation, in a specific field (abortion), of a general right recognised for medical professions under the principle of contractual freedom to refuse to give care. According to this principle, *"Outside situations of emergency and the case where he/she would fail to his/her duty of humanity, a doctor has the right to refuse his/her care for professional or personal reasons."*[65] This right applies also to midwives[66] and dentists.[67]

It is necessary, however, to dwell on the particular case of pharmacists and to mention, in this respect, the 2011 judgment of the European Court of Human

---

64 ECHR, *R. R. v. Poland*, n° 27617/04, 26 May 2011, § 206; ECHR, *P. and S. v. Poland*, n° 57375/08, 30 October 2012, § 106.

65 Article 47 of the French Code of medical deontology.

66 Article 28 of the Code of deontology. See also the international code of deontology of midwives.

67 Article 26 of the Code of deontology.

Rights in *Pichon and Sajous v. France*,[68] since in this case, which stands out as an exception, the Court refused to guarantee the effectiveness of the right to conscientious objection to pharmacists who would escape the national law requiring them to deliver abortion pills. Pursuant to reasoning characterised by positivism, the Court considered that since the selling of the product in question *"is legal and occurs on medical prescription nowhere other than in a pharmacy, the applicants cannot give precedence to their religious beliefs and impose them on others as justification for their refusal to sell such products, since they can manifest those beliefs in many ways outside the professional sphere."*[69] This judgment has been criticised because it unilaterally gave precedence to a simple right over a fundamental freedom, more so by virtue of a schizophrenic notion of freedom of conscience. In order to justify its position, under which the obligation imposed on the pharmacist to deliver abortion pills would affect his freedom of conscience in a limited way only, the Court observed that the pharmacist still had—notwithstanding this obligation—the possibility of acting otherwise, *"outside the professional sphere"*, in keeping to his conscience.[70] But the Court's position would only have been valid if the applicant had been prevented from positively manifesting his beliefs, which was not relevant. In this case, he was forced to act against his beliefs, or face sanctions. The fact of being able to demonstrate against abortion outside the professional sphere reduces in no way the constraint resulting from the obligation to take a direct part in an abortion within the professional sphere.

Nicolas Hervieu rightfully observes that: *"In the case [of] Pichon and Sajous v. France, the "conscientious objection" aspect was totally silenced: the Court's solution would therefore be read back against these new developments (R. R. v. Poland and Bayatyan [v. Armenia]). In my view, if such litigation is laid again before the Court and if the latter follows the logic of its judgments of 2011, it should not so much ensure a balance between two individual claims (freedom of conscience v. obtaining the pill) as check that the State Party itself has taken all necessary measures to ensure this balance (which is definitely different). The European case law will check that despite the wish of a health professional to exercise his/her right of conscientious objection, the global organisation of the health system on the given*

68 ECHR, *Pichon and Sajous v. France*, n° 49853/99, 2 October 2001.

69 *Idem.*

70 J. Raynaud, "Pharmacists cannot put forward their religious beliefs as a reason to refuse to sell contraceptive pills", *JCP E 2002*, n° 1045.

territory nevertheless allows the patients to have access to health services to which they are entitled according to the applicable legislation."[71]

This ECtHR's judgment remains an isolated and old example and does not challenge the general consensus which emerged in favour of an effective right to conscientious objection as regards abortion. Beyond that, it should be noted that since there is a recognition of a right to conscientious objection in the face of abortion, the means (surgical or chemical) by which the abortion is performed should have no relevance.

As to the right for a health institution (excluding, this time, a doctor or a midwife) to refuse the performance of abortions within its premises, the former European Commission on Human Rights recognised and guaranteed this right back in 1989, in the wake of a case involving the decision of a Catholic institution to dismiss one of its employees for having expressed in the press his opinion in favour of abortion.[72] To reach this conclusion, the Commission based its position on respect for the principle of the institutional autonomy of communities and religious institutions, a right guaranteed by virtue of freedom of conscience and religion combined with freedom of association.

Such a solution is similarly retained by several national laws and international organisations. For instance, in a 2010 resolution relating to the *"right to conscientious objection in lawful medical care"*, the Parliamentary Assembly of the Council of Europe asserted that:

> *No person, hospital or institution shall be coerced, held liable or discriminated against in any manner because of a refusal to perform, accommodate, assist or submit to an abortion, the performance of a human miscarriage, or euthanasia or any act which could cause the death of a human foetus or embryo, for any reason.*[73]

This resolution recognises that the right not to collaborate in the voluntary death of a human exceeds the scope of abortion and relates to any biomedical action, at any stage of human life.

---

71 N. Hervieu, discussion of the article "Conscientious objection as examined by the European Court of Human Rights", August 2011, on the blog http://thomasmore.wordpress.com.

72 European Commission on Human Rights, *Rommelfanger v. Federal Republic of Germany*, n° 12242/86, 6 September 1989.

73 PACE, Resolution 1763 (2010) of 7 October 2010, *The right to conscientious objection in lawful medical care.*

Lastly, and beyond the question of abortion, it should be noted that as early as 1989, the *ad hoc* committee of experts on progress in the biomedical sciences (CAHBI, which became CDBI, then DH-BIO) laid down the principle according to which: *"No person may be compelled or required to take a direct part in the performance of acts mentioned in the present principles to which he/she has an objection on the grounds of conscience"* (Principe 3).[74] The acts concerned are *"the techniques of human artificial procreation, in particular to artificial insemination, to the methods involving the removal of ova such as in vitro fertilisation, as well as methods that involve donation of semen, ova or embryos and to acts and procedures on embryos made possible by these techniques."*[75] In this regard, the French legislation, like other national laws, implicitly recognises this right to carry out research on the embryo,[76] which is a real right to conscientious objection, as far as biomedicine is concerned.

c Refusal to Swear on the Gospels

The European Court of Human Rights has recognised that an elected person may rightfully refuse to swear on texts of a religious nature in the name of his conscience:[77] in *Buscarini and others v. San Marino*,[78] the Court examined the case of several deputies forced to swear on the Gospels to be able to take office, and it considered that such an obligation violated Article 9 of ECHR, since its effect was to force elected members of the people to pledge their allegiance to a given religion against their beliefs.

d Refusal to Attend Religious Education Classes or to Take Part in Religious Activities

The European Court of Human Rights also guarantees any person the right to object to his participation (or his minor children's participation) in the activities of a religious community when these activities run against his beliefs. Therefore, it has decided that humanist parents have the right to refuse that their children take part in religious education lessons where a knowledge *"incompatible with their own convictions and beliefs"*[79] is taught. This right to

74 Ad hoc Committee of experts on bioethics (CAHBI), *Principles set out in the report of the Ad Hoc Committee of Experts on Progress in the Biomedical Sciences*, Council of Europe, 1989.

75 *Idem.*

76 Article L2151–7–1 of the French Code of public health.

77 ECHR, *Alexandridis v. Greece*, n° 19516, 21 February 2008.

78 ECHR, *Buscarini and others v. San Marino*, GC, § 34.

79 ECHR, *Folgerø and others v. Norway*, GC, n° 15472/02, 29 June 2007, § 97.

objection is based on the obligation of the State to respect, while exercising its functions in the field of education and teaching, *"the right of parents to ensure such education and teaching in conformity with their own religious and philosophical convictions."*[80] Such a right, which is based on their *"natural duty towards their children",*[81] aims also *"to avoid a situation where pupils face a conflict between the religious education given by the school and the religious or philosophical convictions of their parents."*[82] Indeed, if children are not old enough to reason on their own, they cannot hold their own religious and moral beliefs. Naturally adhering to their parents' beliefs, they too are placed in a situation of two conflicting loyalties (toward parents and toward the school), and the primary nature of filial loyalty should then be respected.[83]

e Refusal to Reveal and Express One's Beliefs

The Human Rights Committee is not the only body to recognise that *"In accordance with articles 18.2 and 17, no one can be compelled to reveal his thoughts or adherence to a religion or belief."*[84] In *Dimitras and others v. Greece,*[85] the ECtHR recognised the same right concerning witnesses involved in a legal procedure. Indeed, in this case, the Greek legislation required the witnesses to reveal their beliefs if they wished to be exempted from the obligation to swear on the Gospels. The Court made the same judgment concerning the refusal by a lawyer to reveal, when taking a professional oath in Greece, that he was not an Orthodox Christian.[86] Lastly, in a case involving Turkey (about stating one's religion on an identity card), the Court clearly held *"that the right to manifest one's religion or beliefs also has a negative aspect, namely an individual's right not to be obliged to disclose his or her religion or beliefs and not to be obliged to act in such a way that it is possible to conclude that he or she holds—or does not hold—such beliefs. Consequently, State authorities are not entitled to intervene in the sphere of an individual's freedom of conscience and to seek to discover his or her religious beliefs or oblige him or her to disclose such beliefs."*[87]

---

80 First additional Protocol to ECHR (1952), Article 2 and Article 18.4 of the Covenant of 1966.

81 ECHR, *Hassan and Eylem Zengin v. Turkey*, n° 1448/04, judgment of 9 October 2007, § 50.

82 ECHR, *Hassan and Eylem Zengin v. Turkey*, n° 1448/04, judgment of 9 October 2007, § 71.

83 ECHR, *Dojan and others v. Germany*, n° 319/08 . . ., decision of 13 September 2011. The Court underlined that the Convention did not guarantee the right not to be confronted with opinions that were opposed to one's own convictions.

84 General Comment n° 22, *pre-cited.*

85 ECHR, *Dimitras and others v. Greece*, n° 42837/06, 3237/07, 3269/07, 35793/07 and 6099/08, 3 June 2010.

86 ECHR, *Alexandridis v. Greece*, n° 19516/06, 21 February 2008.

87 ECHR, *Sinan Işık v. Turkey*, n° 21924/05, 2 February 2010, § 41.

The right recognised in this case extends beyond conscientious objection, since it guarantees the right of a person not to express his beliefs in the *forum externum*. This right, recognised in the framework of a society impregnated with religion (like Greece), should theoretically be reversible and also benefit to persons who, living in a secularised society, do not wish to be forced to reveal their moral or religious beliefs if those have become 'politically incorrect'.

f Refusal to Celebrate the Union of Two Persons of the Same Sex

The case of *Eweida and others v. United Kingdom*[88] was, *inter alia*, about the dismissal of a town hall employee (Mrs Ladele) and of a relationship counsellor (Mr McFarlane) following their refusals, based on their religious beliefs, respectively, to register civil unions of same-sex partners and to provide psycho-sexual counselling to such partners. The ECtHR admitted that the applicants' refusal fell within the scope of freedom of conscience and religion (§ 103), that it was a manifestation of their beliefs and that it therefore benefited from the protection of freedom of conscience and religion. The Court concluded that *"[t]he State's positive obligation under Article 9 required it to secure his* [McFarlane] *rights under Article 9."* (§ 108). However, in both cases, the Court considered that the sanction imposed on the applicants was not disproportionate, after having noted that the United Kingdom had a wide margin of appreciation to balance the competing rights (§ 106 and 109), with the legitimate aim of ensuring the smooth working of the service and of respecting the employer's policy which was to promote equality and fight discrimination (§ 105 and 109). Nonetheless, despite the recognition of the wide discretion available to member States, the very principle according to which a (limitable) right to conscientious objection exists was indeed recognised in this case.

g Refusal to Allow Hunting

The refusal to allow hunting on private land bears witness to the variety of cases with which jurisdictions may be confronted. In this regard, the ECtHR implicitly recognised, in substance, the right to conscientious objection, but did not express itself as regards Article 9 of ECHR. Indeed, concerning a case where an individual refused to accommodate hunters on land belonging to him, the Court stated the following principle: *"To compel a person by law to join an association* [a hunting association] *such that it is fundamentally contrary to his own convictions to be a member of it, and to oblige him, on account of his membership of that association, to transfer his rights over the land he owns so that the association in question can attain objectives of which he disapproves,*

88 ECHR, *Eweida and others v. United Kingdom*, n° 48420/10, 15 January 2013.

goes beyond what is necessary to ensure that a fair balance is struck between conflicting interests and cannot be considered proportionate to the aim pursued."[89] Even if the Court found in this case a violation of the right of ownership, its reasoning indicates that the constraints bore first on the applicants' beliefs, hence on their freedom of conscience. By law n° 2000–698 of 26th of July 2000, France recognised the right to oppose a hunt on one's land *"in the name of competing personal beliefs"*.

h Refusal of Vaccination

According to the former European Commission on Human Rights, *"A requirement to undergo a vaccination does not constitute an interference with the freedom protected by this Article (9) since it applies to everyone regardless of their religion or personal convictions."*[90] This argument is not convincing and might even be used by a State wishing to oppose any objection to military service, under the pretext that such obligation *"applies to everybody"*. That an obligation is of a general nature does not mean it cannot affect freedom of conscience. On the other hand, the Court considered, in the case of *Salvetti v. Italy*,[91] that compulsory vaccination as a non-voluntary medical treatment interferes with the right to respect for private life guaranteed by Article 8 § 1 of the European Convention. A new application invoking Article 9 is presently pending.[92] On the national level, numerous countries recognize the ability to object to vaccination; such was the case as early as 1898 in the United Kingdom[93] and seemed to be the origin of the notion of conscientious objection.[94]

Given the importance and complexity of this question, coupled with the differences of views within the Human Rights Committee and the recurring weakness of the argument used by Strasbourg authorities, there is a need to further the understanding of conscientious objection and to develop evaluation criteria for it. This would respond to the questions asked by Sir Nigel

---

89 ECHR, *Chassagnou and others v. France*, GC, § 117. See also *Schneider v. Luxembourg*, n° 2113/04, 10 July 2007, § 82.

90 European Commission on Human Rights, *Boffa and others v. San Marino*, dec. n° 26536/95, 15 January 1998.

91 ECHR, *Salvetti v. Italy*, n° 42197/98, 9 July 2002.

92 ECHR, *Vavricka v. Czech Republic*, n° 47621/13.

93 A. Bertrand and D. Torn. *Libertés individuelles et santé collective. Une étude socio-historique de l'obligation vaccinale.* Cermes—Rapport au Conseil supérieur d'hygiène publique de France, Novembre 2004, 108 pages.

94 High Commissioner for Human Rights, *"Conscientious Objection to Military Service"*, HR/PUB/12/1, United Nations, 2012, p. 4.

Rodley, Mr Krister Thelin and Mr Cornelis Flinterman[95]—among others—as well as to similar question asked by Mr Walter Kälin who wished to know *"what are the criteria to distinguish between manifestations of belief worthy of absolute protection and those expressions of one's beliefs that may be limited"*.[96]

III Evaluation Criteria of Conscientious Objection

As the Human Rights Committee notes, *"the right to freedom of conscience does not as such imply the right to refuse all obligations imposed by law, nor does it provide immunity from criminal liability in respect of every such refusal."*[97] Given the wide variety of situations—from the most serious to the most fanciful—leading to a refusal of obedience, public authorities, and especially judges, have a difficult task, since all refusals of obedience cannot be said to be motivated by conscientious objection. This is a tricky aspect of analysis; how are we to distinguish—among all refusals—those which deserve to benefit from the protection of freedom of conscience and religion, knowing that public authorities must refrain from making a judgment on the beliefs themselves? Here again, objective and subjective approaches coexist: objection should be appreciated as regards both the nature of the act objected to (objective approach) and the quality of the belief of the objector (subjective approach).

This third part, therefore, seeks to reveal the rationality of the concept of conscientious objection and to identify the objective criteria of appreciation, without directly judging the validity of the beliefs in question. Such criteria can in fact be useful to public authorities in order to recognize a fair degree of protection for an objection, according to the circumstances of every case.

Based on the philosophy of the concept of conscientious objection and on the case law of the European Court, we propose to determine:

- whether the refusal comes from a reasonable person;
- whether the situation implies the positive freedom (power to act) or the negative freedom (not being obliged to act) of conscience and religion;
- whether the objection originates in simple personal conveniences or in a prescription of conscience;

95 Concurring individual opinion of Sir Nigel Rodley, Mr Krister Thelin and Mr Cornelis Flinterman in HRC, *Cenk Atasoy and others v. Turkey*, 2012, mentioned above.

96 Separate opinion in HRC, *Jong-nam Kim and others v. Republic of Korea*, 2012, mentioned above.

97 HRC, *Paul Westerman v. Netherlands*, Communication n° 682/1996, § 9.3.

- whether conscientious objection obeys moral or religious prescriptions; and
- whether there is proximity between the act and the objection's content.[98]

1 *Distinguishing whether the Refusal Comes from a Reasonable Person*

Given its nature, conscientious objection necessarily involves the personal behaviour of an individual who has the use of reason. A person who has not yet acquired (e.g. a child) or no more enjoys (e.g. a madman) the use of reason would be strictly unable to exercise a true conscientious objection.

Conscientious objection, therefore, cannot be asserted by an association of persons, because a community does not have reason. The former European Commission on Human Rights seemed to favour this view when it declared in 1988: *"Insofar as Article 9 is concerned, the Commission considers that a distinction must be made in this respect between the freedom of conscience and the freedom of religion, which can also be exercised by a church as such."*[99] This does not mean, however, that an association is deprived of protection: in the name of freedom of association combined with freedom of conscience and religion perceived in its collective dimension, an association can refuse to participate in acts opposed to its *ethos*. This is guaranteed by the "right to autonomy" of institutions founded on moral or religious beliefs, which forms part of the freedoms of association and of religion perceived in its collective dimension. In this regard, the European Court of Human Rights considered that *"[t]he autonomous existence of religious communities is indispensable for pluralism in a democratic society and is thus an issue at the very heart of the protection which Article 9 of the Convention affords"* and that *"[i]t has a direct interest, not only for*

98 In their very recent work (Freedom of religion…, *op. cit.*, p. 296 and foll.), MM. Bielefedt and Weiner and Mrs Ghanea briefly suggest a combination of five criteria: 1. the question must be a morally grave one ("gravity of the moral concern"); 2. The person's conscience must categorically oppose any personal participation ("situation of conscientious veto"); 3. The question must be about a constitutive aspect of the very person's identity ("connectedness to an identity shaping principled belief"); 4. The objector must be forced to proximately collaborate in the action objected to (*"level of complicity in the requested action"*); 5. The objector must accept to perform an alternative service (*"willingness to perform an alternative service"*). These criteria partially coincide with those we propose. The third criterion seems to duplicate the second; as to the fifth, it seems to qualify not the objection itself, but the attitude of the objector.

99 Com. Eur. HR, *Verein Kontakt-Information-Therapie and Siegfried Hagen v. Austria*, n° 11921/86, 12 October 1988, *DR* 57, § 96–97.

the actual organisation of those communities but also for the effective enjoyment by all their active members of the right to freedom of religion."[100]

This possibility, that groups may refuse to perform certain practices opposed to their beliefs, is also admitted in—among others—the *guidelines* of the Organisation for the Security and Cooperation in Europe (OSCE), which recognized that "[*t*]*here are many circumstances where individuals and groups, as a matter of conscience, find it difficult or morally objectionable to comply with laws of general applicability*". Likewise, the Parliamentary Assembly of the Council of Europe recently reaffirmed on several occasions this principle of autonomy, especially in its resolutions 1928 of 2013[101] and 1728 of 2010[102] in which it urges the member States to create the possibility to "*grant exemptions to religious institutions and organisations when such institutions and organisations are either engaging in religious activities or when legal requirements conflict with tenets of religious belief and doctrine, or would require such institutions and organisations to forfeit any portion of their religious autonomy.*" (art. 17). Likewise, the Council Directive 2000/78/EC of 27 November 2000, establishing a general framework for equal treatment in employment and occupation,[103] ensures the protection of the *ethos* of churches and organisations whose ethics are based on religion or beliefs.

This question is particularly important regarding the ability of institutions to oppose the practice of abortion or euthanasia on their premises. So, in a decision of 6 September 1989 rendered in *Rommelfanger v. Federal Republic of Germany*,[104] the former European Commission on Human Rights recognized the right of a Catholic hospital to demand its employees, on the basis of their duty of loyalty toward the Church, to refrain from publicly speaking in favour of abortion. It therefore considered that non-compliance with this obligation could justify the dismissal of the employee concerned. It may be deduced from this decision, *mutatis mutandis*, that an institution founded on beliefs opposed to abortion would have a right to refuse being compelled to practise it. In any

100 ECHR, *Fernandez-Martinez v. Spain*, GC, n° 56030/07, 12 June 2014, § 127.

101 PACE, Resolution 1928 (2013), *Safeguarding human rights in relation to religion and belief, and protecting religious communities from violence*, art. 9.13.

102 PACE, Resolution 1728 (2010), *Discrimination on the basis of sexual orientation and gender identity.*

103 Council Directive 2000/78/EC, 27 November 2000 establishing a general framework for equal treatment in employment and occupation.

104 European Commission on Human Rights, *Rommelfanger v. Federal Republic of Germany*, mentioned above.

case, this right is largely recognized by national legislation, as well as by PACE in a resolution of 2010.[105]

2 *Distinguishing between Positive Manifestation and Negative Expression of Freedom of Conscience*

Sir Nigel Rodley notes that *"freedom of thought, conscience and religion embraces the right not to manifest, as well as the right to manifest, one's conscientiously held beliefs"*.[106] Likewise, for Judge Paulo Pinto de Albuquerque: *"[t]he ambit of the right to conscientious objection includes not only the freedom to act according to one's beliefs, but also the freedom not to act, not to associate and not to tolerate actions from others which contradict one's personal convictions"*.[107] So this freedom, like any other freedom,[108] has two sides. The first one, positive, consists in not being prevented from acting according to one's conscience: it is a positive manifestation (in the *forum externum*). The second one, negative, consists in not being compelled to act against one's conscience: it gives rise to a negative manifestation.

Even if both sides of this freedom result from the synderesis, since the manifestation of a conviction leads to accomplishing something good (positive manifestation) or to avoiding doing something evil (negative manifestation), the distinction to be made between the two is important. This is because it is not the same to be prevented from doing something good prescribed by conscience as to be compelled to do something evil reproved by conscience.

a Positive and Negative Manifestations of Freedom of Conscience

i *Positive Manifestation of Freedom of Conscience (or Positive Freedom)*

This *positive* freedom is related to the faculty of manifesting one's beliefs by external acts. Article 9 of the ECHR enumerates the different forms of manifestation: worship, teaching, practice and observance (rites). As they can affect competing rights and interests, they are subjected to the compulsions and

---

105 PACE, Resolution 1763 (2010).

106 Individual opinion of Committee member Sir Nigel Rodley, jointly with members Mr. Krister Thelin and Mr. Cornelis Flinterman (concurring) in *Cenk Atasoy v. Turkey*, 2012, mentioned above.

107 Partly concurring and partly dissenting opinion of Judge Pinto de Albuquerque in *Herrmann v. Germany*, GC, mentioned above.

108 Freedoms of association, marriage or expression have also a negative side which guarantees the rights not to to associate, not to marry and not to express oneself.

limits inherent to any positive freedom.[109] Such restrictions forbid anyone to do all or part of the good to which his conscience is inclined. Moreover, the ECtHR specifies that *"Article 9 does not protect every act motivated or inspired by a religion or belief"*.[110] It does not always guarantee the right to act in a manner dictated by a belief, and it does not confer upon individuals acting in this way the right to escape rules which prove justified.[111] Such is the case, for instance, of assisted suicide,[112] pre-nubile religious marriage,[113] or the distribution of tracts.[114]

Refusing to respect a prohibition to act according to one's beliefs, which then takes the form of an action positively manifesting these beliefs, enters the scope of this common regime of freedom to positively manifest one's beliefs. Such is the case, for instance, of a person who wears a forbidden religious sign (religious belief) or who accommodates out of altruism an immigrant in an irregular situation despite the prohibition to do so (moral conviction). Such was the case, too, of Antigone who defied Creon's prohibition (both moral and religious conviction).

ii *Negative Dimension of Freedom of Conscience* (*or Negative Freedom*)

Freedom of conscience also has a negative dimension protecting a person from the obligation to act against his conscience. A well-known form is the *"freedom (...) not to hold religious beliefs and (...) not to practise a religion"*.[115] Most often, this negative freedom is perceived as the freedom of *"atheists, agnostics, sceptics and the unconcerned"*;[116] in fact, it is the freedom of minorities faced with the dominant discourse and power. This negative dimension of freedom of

109 Public security, protection of public order, health or moral, or protection of other persons' rights and freedoms.

110 *Hassan and Tchaouch v. Bulgaria*, GC, n° 30985/96, 26 October 2000, § 60; *Kalaç v. Turkey*, n° 32323/96, dec. 1 July 1997, § 27; *Metropolitan Church of Bessarabia and others v. Moldova*, n° 45701/99, 13 December 2001, § 117.

111 *Leyla Şahin v. Turkey*, GC, n° 44774/98, 10 November 2005, § 121.

112 *Pretty v. UK*, n° 2346/02, 29 April 2002.

113 European Commission on Human Rights, *Khan v. UK*, n° 11579/85, dec., 7 July 1986.

114 European Commission on Human Rights, *Arrowsmith v. UK*, n° 7050/75, dec., 12 October 1978; European Commission on Human Rights, *Van Den Dungen v. Netherlands*, n° 22838/93, dec., 22 February 1995.

115 *Buscarini and others v. San Marino*, GC, n° 24645/94, 18 February 1999, § 43; *Refah Partisi and others v. Turkey*, GC, n° 41340/98..., 13 February 2003, § 90.

116 Leitmotiv of the Court, especially in *Bayatyan*, § 118.

conscience is illustrated by the refusal to take a religious oath,[117] to participate in a religious class or indoctrination,[118] or to work during the Shabbat[119] and on Sunday.[120]

Negative freedom aims at preserving not the positive *manifestation* of a belief, but the integrity of conscience itself, as the unity between intelligence and will which characterizes human nature. Whereas there is a difference in quality between a conviction and its positive manifestation, since the latter is the material realisation of a conceptual belief (the philosophers would speak of the *actuation* of the conviction), such a difference does not exist between a conviction and its negative manifestation: it is the same refusal to act.

Then, a "conviction not to do" does not spontaneously come from the *forum internum*, the inner self; and it does not need to manifest itself in the *forum externum* to be respected. As an illustration, if your convictions condemn theft, you can respect them without showing it. So, most of the time, negative manifestations go unnoticed, since they are mere abstentions. A 'conviction not to do' will only externally manifest itself if the subject is ordered by someone to act against it and if he refuses to do so. The subject is then forced to disclose his belief, and his refusal is a negative manifestation of it. For certain persons, the obligation to disclose their belief already amounts to a violation of their *forum internum* and consequently of their freedom of conscience.[121]

iii *Differences in the Scope of Interference Depending on whether it Aims at a Positive or Negative Manifestation*

When a positive manifestation of belief is restricted, such restriction concerns the extent of this manifestation, not the belief itself.[122] On the other hand, when a negative manifestation is restricted, such restriction concerns the belief itself, since there is an identity between the negative manifestation and the belief. Now, as it is materially possible to prevent a subject from accomplishing a part of the good he is convinced to do, it is likewise impossible to force the same subject to act—even only partially—against his belief. Indeed,

117 ECHR, *Buscarini and others v. San Marino; Alexandridis v. Greece*, n° 19516/06, 21 February 2008, *Dimitras and others v. Greece*, n° 42837/06 . . ., 3 June 2010.

118 ECHR, *Dojan and others v. Germany*, dec., n° 319/08.

119 ECHR, *Francesco Sessa v. Italy*, n° 28790/08, 3 April 2012.

120 European Commission on Human Rights, *Konttinen v. Finland*, n° 24949/94, dec., 3 December 1996, European Commission on Human Rights, *Stedman v. United Kingdom*, dec., n° 29107/95, 9 April 1997.

121 See, for instance, the opinion of Walter Kälin in *Jong-nam Kim and others v. Republic of Korea*, mentioned above. We find this position excessive.

122 Unless any manifestation of the belief is forbidden.

interference in the positive dimension of freedom of conscience can always be modulated, limited and proportioned to circumstances, whereas this cannot be done with the negative dimension.

When you forbid someone to act in line with his conscience, you prevent him from realising all or part of a 'good' recommended by his conscience. On the other hand, when you force someone to act against his conscience, you oblige him to commit an 'evil', i.e. an act reproved by his conscience. In other words, restricting a positive manifestation affects the material realisation (the actuation) of the belief by limiting it, for example, to certain places and times. By contrast, forcing someone to do evil does not affect the realisation of the belief, but affects the belief itself. A good can be done partially, but an evil is always total, even if it can be reduced. Evil is a question of principle, while good is a question of measure: I cannot steal, not even one euro (principle), but I can donate 20, 50 or 100 euros (measure). There is no symmetry between good and evil.[123]

Moreover, only a positive manifestation can be subject to restrictions or limitations, while a negative manifestation (a refusal to act) cannot materially be subject to restrictions or limitations—but it can be compelled or punished.

For instance, whereas it is possible to modulate, according to place and time, an interference with the positive dimension of freedom of conscience represented by the prohibition to wear the veil, such can never be the case for an interference with the negative dimension of freedom of conscience consisting in forcing a woman to wear it. A woman's freedom of conscience is totally violated when she is forced to wear the veil, whether for just a day or a year.[124] If human rights can tolerate a limitation of the ability to wear the veil,[125] because it is a manifestation of beliefs, human rights cannot tolerate that a woman be forced to act against her beliefs by wearing it.

The result of this difference in the scope of the interference, depending on whether the interference concerns a positive or negative manifestation, is that

123 St. Thomas Aquinas synthesizes this difference between positive and negative prescriptions by stating that the first oblige *"Semper sed non ad semper"*, while the second oblige *"Semper sed ad semper"*. Cf. François Knittel, *Préceptes affirmatifs et préceptes négatifs chez saint Thomas d'Aquin*, Clovis, 2012.

124 This is how evil is always a totality in itself, even if it can be reduced in duration or in intensity.

125 See, among others, ECHR, *Dahlab v. Switzerland*, dec., n° 42393/98; ECHR, *SAS v. France*, n° 43835/11, 1 July 2014; *Leyla Şahin*, mentioned above; *Köse and others v. Turkey*, dec., n° 26625/02, 7 December 2010; *Kervanci v. France*, n° 31645/04, 4 December 2008; *Aktas v. France*, dec., n° 43563/08, 30 June 2009; *Ranjit Singh v. France*, dec., n° 27561/08, 30 June 2009.

it is more serious to force somebody to act against his conscience than to prevent him from acting in line with his conscience. In this sense, the European Court judged that the prohibition to wear the veil in school, during a security check,[126] or on identity photographs intended for official documents,[127] does not violate Article 9, provided that the necessity of such prohibition is established.

It is true that an abstention resulting from the refusal to execute an order is in itself a form of action. It can be sustained, like the ECtHR, that to refuse selling an abortion pill or bearing arms is an external manifestation of beliefs,[128] and that this voluntary abstention (negative manifestation) can have consequences for other people and thus be blameworthy. Nevertheless, this negative manifestation of freedom of conscience and religion[129] is not equivalent to a positive manifestation and so should be treated differently by civil authorities. Negative freedom deserves a higher degree of protection, because it is far more serious, as has been said, to force somebody to act against his beliefs than to prevent him from acting according to them.

b Consequences of such Distinction

The difference described above between negative and positive manifestation of freedom of conscience makes it possible to grasp more fully the reasons why conscientious objection is generally understood as concerning only the refusal of acting against one's beliefs.

So, any action which aims at compelling somebody (who has the use of reason and capacity for discernment) to change his belief affects the *forum internum* (the inner self) of the subject and represents a violation of his freedom of conscience absolutely guaranteed both by Article 18, paragraph 1 of the Covenant and Article 9, paragraph 1 (first part of the sentence) of ECHR.[130] Thus, when public authorities are confronted with a conscientious objection, they cannot legitimately undertake to force the subject to change his belief, for instance by subjecting him to any form of moral re-education, when this person has sufficient reason to hold beliefs. Furthermore, compelling someone to act positively against his beliefs would constitute violence, and sometimes even an injustice. But in some cases, society has grounds for punishing a

126 ECHR, *Phull v. France*, dec., n° 35753/03, 11 January 2005; *El Morsli v. France*, dec., n° 15585/06, 4 March 2008.

127 *Mann Singh v. France*, dec., n° 24479/07, 13 November 2008.

128 *Bayatyan*, § 112.

129 Or this manifestation of freedom of conscience and religion in its negative dimension.

130 Judge Fischbach, separate opinion in *Chassagnou v. France*.

person because of his refusal to act, since it may so happen that this refusal unduly affects the rights of others. Simply put, freedom of conscience does not confer complete impunity on the conscientious objector.

When a person sanctioned for having objected brings his case before a judge, the latter must determine whether the subject has been compelled to change his beliefs or if he has been sanctioned exclusively for these beliefs; if such has been the case, this constitutes a direct violation of the Convention. But if such has not been the case, it is up to the judge to establish whether the sanction imposed on the objector because of his refusal was—in the circumstances of the case—legitimate and necessary in terms of the respect due to freedom of conscience.[131]

This being said, all refusals to execute an order do not necessarily express a 'conviction'. A conviction is not an opinion. How are we to judge whether the motive of a refusal is a conviction within the meaning of Article 9 of the ECHR? New distinctions are therefore necessary in this respect.

3 *Distinguishing between "Convictions" and "Personal Conveniences"*

Though the United Nations Commission on Human Rights recognized that conscientious objection *"derives from principles and reasons of conscience, including profound beliefs, arising from religious, moral, ethical, humanitarian or similar motives"*,[132] it is not always easy to establish if, in this or that particular case, the *motive of the objection* does constitute a 'belief' within the meaning of Article 9 of the ECHR and, as such, deserves the protection granted to freedom of conscience and religion, and if the objection itself is of a serious nature.

In this regard, the quality of the conviction in the name of which the subject expressed his objection is distinct from the quality of the objection. For instance, a cult-motivated alimentary prescription is assuredly related to a religious belief and therefore deserves to be protected as such. But does the subject who pretends to object on such a basis really act on the basis of commitment to this belief? Is he not motivated by something else?[133]

Several criteria can be derived from the European Court's case law and from the conclusions of the Human Rights Committee in order to evaluate the quality both of the beliefs invoked and of the objection expressed. Thanks to these criteria, it is possible to separate convictions which '*are worthy of respect in a*

131 *Bayatyan v. Armenia*, § 10.

132 Commission on Human Rights: Resolution 1998/77, 22 April 1998, § 10.

133 For example, a detained person who invokes beliefs in order to enjoy a special diet.

"democratic society"'[134] from the simple *'opinions'*, which are more related to the regime of Article 8.

a Evaluation Criteria for the Quality of Beliefs (of the Motive of the Objection)

The ECtHR noticed that not all opinions or convictions fall within the scope of Article 9 § 1 of the Convention.[135] It is possible to establish four successive criteria for the evaluation of the quality of beliefs.

First, the beliefs must be *"genuinely-held religious beliefs"*,[136] according to the Human Rights Committee, or *"deeply and genuinely held religious or other beliefs"*,[137] according to the Court of Strasbourg. The belief can be of an *'ethical'* nature[138] (i.e. moral) or of a *'religious'* nature.[139]

Secondly, the content of beliefs must be identifiable.[140] The ECtHR states in this regard that *"The term 'conviction', taken on its own, is not synonymous with the words 'opinions' and 'ideas'. It denotes views that attain a certain level of cogency, seriousness, cohesion and importance"*.[141] Atheism and pacifism are among philosophical convictions.

Thirdly, when they are of a religious nature, beliefs must be linked to a *"known religion"*,[142] even if *"The right to freedom of religion as guaranteed under the Convention excludes any discretion on the part of the State to determine whether religious beliefs or the means used to express such beliefs are legitimate."*[143] So, when the judge is able to find that a belief at the source of an objection is part of the cult-related precepts of a given religion, he cannot in principle evaluate its relevance.

---

134 ECHR, *Campbell and Cosans v. UK*, n°s 7511/76 & 7743/76, 25 February 1982, § 36.

135 ECHR, *Enver Aydemir v. Turkey*, n° 26012/11, 7 May 2016.

136 See, for instance, HRC, *Yeo-Bum Yoon and Mr. Myung-Jin Choi v. Republic of Korea*, § 8.3.

137 ECHR, *Bayatyan v. Armenia*, § 110.

138 ECHR, *Chassagnou v. France*, § 114 and *Schneider v. Luxembourg*, § 80, mentioned above.

139 ECHR, *Eweida and others v. UK*, § 108.

140 European Commission on Human Rights, *T. Mac Feeley v. United Kingdom*, 15 May 1980, DR 20/44.

141 ECHR, *Folgerø and others v. Norway*, GC, n° 15472/02, 29 June 2007, § 84; see also ECHR, *Valsamis v. Greece*, n° 21787/93, 18 December 1996, §§ 25 and 27 and ECHR, *Campbell and Cosans vs United Kingdom*, n° 7511/76, 7743/76, 25 February 1982, §§ 36 and 37.

142 ECHR, *Valsamis v. Greece*, § 26.

143 ECHR, *Manoussakis and others v. Greece*, n° 18748/91, 26 September 1996, § 47; *Hassan and Tchaouch v. Bulgaria*, GC, n° 30985/96, 26 October 2000, § 78; *Refah Partisi and others v. Turkey*, GC, § 91.

Fourthly, when the beliefs are not of a religious nature, *"the expression 'philosophical convictions'* [...] *denotes* [...] *such convictions* [that] *are worthy of respect in a 'democratic society'* [...] *and are not incompatible with human dignity".*[144] Not only is this reference to democracy and the dignity of the person useful in itself, but it expresses the link—constitutive of human nature—between the personal conscience and the common sense of what is just and good.

What philosophical beliefs have in common with religious beliefs and what differentiates them from moral convictions is that they are not directly related to justice.

b Evaluation Criteria for the Quality of the Objection

The ECtHR distinguishes the objection from its ethical or religious motives, i.e. from the conviction invoked to sustain it. It is not sufficient that the objection be founded on religious or moral beliefs: in addition, the objection itself should also bear the characteristics of a belief.

The ECtHR, therefore, has decided that the objection itself must bear the characteristics of *"a conviction or belief of sufficient cogency, seriousness, cohesion and importance to attract the guarantees of Article 9."*[145] A person objecting only intermittently or out of opportunism would not deserve the protection of this provision. Such could be the case of a hospital doctor objecting to the performance of an abortion in the hospital only, but not in his private practice, or of a person objecting in the name of a cult-related prescription of a religion that he does not seriously practice. The subject must be consistent. That said, the right to change beliefs is protected too, so that anyone can become an objector to a practice that he would have accepted before. A soldier, whether drafted or even professional, can object after his enlistment,[146] though he previously accepted the bearing of arms. Also, the fact that doctors, pharmacists or midwifes have voluntarily chosen their profession does not allow questioning the quality of their objection or depriving them of protection[147] as regards a particular act.

The objection should result from a *"serious and insurmountable conflict"*[148] *"between the obligation* [...] *and a person's conscience or his deeply and*

---

144 ECHR, *Campbell and Cosans v. United Kingdom*, § 36.

145 *Bayatyan v. Armenia*, § 110. It refers to its judgment in *Campbell and Cosans v. United Kingdom* and, *a contrario*, to its judgement in *Pretty v. United Kingdom*, § 82.

146 HRC, Conclusions on Kazakhstan, CCPR/C/KAZ/CO/1, § 23. See also H. Bielefeldt et al., *op. cit.*, p. 277.

147 H. Bielefedt et al., *op. cit.*, p. 301.

148 *Batyatyan v. Armenia*, § 110.

genuinely held religious or other beliefs".[149] So, the conflict must satisfy two criteria, first its seriousness, then its insurmountability. As to the first (seriousness), it must be understood as requiring that the matter is not a minor one but one which bears weight on the conscience. Such is not the case, for instance, with the general obligation to pay taxes.[150] As to the second criterion (insurmountability), this means that the objection should be the only option available to the subject, who must be cornered into refusal, without any loophole left to him. Ever since the *Ladele* case,[151] the ECtHR, reversing its previous case law,[152] considers that a conflict of conscience in a professional setting enjoys the protection of Article 9, even if the employee has freely chosen his employment and if he has the possibility of resigning. It stated that *"the better approach would be to weigh* [the possibility of changing jobs] *in the overall balance when considering whether the restriction* [of freedom of conscience] *was proportionate".*[153] So, the possibility for an employee to resign does not deprive the objection of its insurmountable character. Heiner Bielefeldt, Special Rapporteur of the United Nations on freedom of religion or belief, underlines in this sense that *"by signing an employment contract employees do not waive their freedom of thought, conscience, religion, or belief."*[154] Likewise, the Parliamentary Assembly of the Council of Europe called on the member States to *"uphold freedom of conscience in the workplace while ensuring that access to services provided by law is maintained and the right of others to be free from discrimination is protected".*[155] Assuredly, it would be unreasonable for a religious Muslim to seek employment in a pig-breeding farm, but the situation is different with an objecting doctor, since abortion and euthanasia are exceptional practices which depart from the therapeutic goal of medicine. Otherwise, persons refusing to cooperate in the voluntary death of a human being would be prevented from exercising medical professions.

Finally, the objection should not be based on *"reasons of personal benefit or convenience but on the ground of his genuinely held religious convictions".*[156] This criterion of personal disinterestedness is enlightening, since it indicates that

---

149 *Idem.*

150 European Commission on Human Rights, *C. v. United Kingdom*, n° 10358/83, dec., 15 December 1983, DR 37, p. 148.

151 ECHR, *Eweida and others v. United Kingdom.*

152 ECHR, *Stedman v. United Kingdom*, mentioned above with regard to an employee who refused to work on Sunday.

153 ECHR, *Eweida and others v. United Kingdom*, § 83.

154 H. Bielefedt et al., *op. cit.*, p. 304.

155 PACE, Resolution 2036 (2015), *Tackling intolerance and discrimination in Europe with a special focus on Christians*, § 6.2.2.

156 ECHR, *Bayatyan v. Armenia*, § 124.

the genuine objector does not act in an "anarchic" spirit, but in obedience to his moral and/or religious beliefs when the law differs from them. Indeed, in order to be consistent, the objector is often obliged to sacrifice his personal interest, especially in the professional field.

c Dealing with Personal Convenience and Other Opinions

Personal positions which do not manifest a belief within the meaning of Article 9, and therefore cannot give rise to a genuine conscientious objection as such, are not for all that devoid of any conventional protection, since the latter can be obtained on the ground of other freedoms, especially when considered through their negative side.

Indeed, all freedoms have a negative side: freedom of expression includes freedom of non-expression, freedom of association includes freedom of non-association, freedom to marry includes freedom not to marry, etc. As an example, when the Court was solicited by a person who was morally opposed to hunting and challenged a sanction inflicted on him because he refused to execute the obligation to join a hunting association and did not tolerate hunting on his property, the Court did not base its decision on the principle of freedom of conscience, but on the principles of freedom of association and freedom of ownership.[157]

More frequently, the ECtHR chooses to decide the matter on the basis of Article 8 of the ECHR, which protects individual autonomy as regards private life. Such was the case, for instance, with requests invoking a right to assisted suicide. Thus, in the case *Pretty v. United Kingdom*,[158] while the applicant availed herself—among other arguments—of her philosophical beliefs in support of her request for assisted suicide (which is a refusal to live), the Court, without questioning the firmness of the applicant's beliefs, excluded them from the ambit of Article 9, paragraph 2 of the Convention and analysed them only from the angle of the person's autonomy.

Such a distinction made between an expression of the autonomy of a person, related to Article 8 of the ECHR, and a manifestation of belief, related to Article 9 of the same Convention, deserves closer attention.[159]

157 ECHR, *Hermann v. Germany*, GC.

158 ECHR, *Pretty v. United Kingdom*.

159 This distinction is difficult, because we often reduce conscience to its psychological dimension detached from its common moral aspect; conscience is then perceived as producing subjective and relative values. Therefore, morality and religion are immersed in a common subjectivism from which every person tries to extract his individuality by affirming choices which would be arbitrary as well as un-questionable.

It would seem, *prima facie*, that these two concepts overlap, since it is through his conscience that a person not only forms his beliefs, but also determines his norms of action (his autonomy). In other words, without conscience, there is no autonomy. In fact, the redactors of the ECHR did not deem it useful or convenient to guarantee (explicitly) a right to "individual autonomy", perhaps because they thought that this right was already covered by the protection of freedom of conscience.

Now, the concept of individual autonomy emerged as and when individualism was asserting itself in Western society. Indeed, such an assertion of individualism developed alongside a change in the common understanding of conscience, especially through the assertion of "the autonomy of conscience", the latter designating a conscience supposed to discover by itself its own beliefs, based on its own moral or religious premises. This is a subjective and relativist conception of moral doing. However, as we have shown before, the criteria for an authentic conscientious objection converge on the principle of the imperative obedience of the person to the prescriptions of his conscience; such prescriptions, we understand, should be related to identified and serious moral or religious beliefs. This is a form of (participated) heteronomy of the objector's conscience which is required in support of his objection's admissibility.

So, the distinction between conviction and personal convenience overlaps the distinction between the heteronomous and the autonomous conceptions of conscience: either conscience is in itself the superior requirement in the name of which the objection is formed, or it is only the instrument for perceiving this requirement. In the first case, we are confronted with an autonomous and subjective conception of conscience, which can then be identified with psyche, with conscience of oneself, which is itself a standard after all. In the second case, we are confronted with an objective or a heteronomous conception of conscience, imperatively prescribing to the person a behaviour which conforms to standards of a moral and possibly religious nature imposing themselves on the conscience and within the conscience.

Ultimately, perhaps the difference between what relates to individual autonomy and what relates to convictions resides in that idea which the person has formed about the required use of reason. Whereas conviction or moral judgment derives from right and enlightened reason, in order to attain an almost scientific quality, individual autonomy does not require proof of its rationality and involves an element of arbitrariness producing individual 'choices' that society need not question. So, while individual autonomy produces 'choices', freedom of conscience produces 'convictions', even if, in practice, both are not mutually exclusive.

Nevertheless, the difference between what relates to individual autonomy, on the one hand, and to conviction, on the other hand, perfectly reflects the difference between Articles 8 and 9 of the Convention. As a matter of fact, Article 8 of the ECHR protects the autonomy of the person on account of private life,[160] i.e. the ability of the subject to find standards for himself, and aims at the realisation of the personal free will, at the self-fulfilment and development of personality.[161] For its part, and in a different way, Article 9 of ECHR supposes a form of heteronomy and refers to the ability of the person to judge in the light of morality and possibly of religion, as well as to comply with the prescriptions of morality and/or religion. However, this is not a complete form of heteronomy, for the existence of conscience requires an internalising process, a participation of the person in applying his moral evaluation to different cases with the whole rigour of reason.

4 *Distinguishing between "Moral Objection" and "Religious Objection"*

Conscientious objection can be analysed further depending on whether the conviction which underlies it is of a moral or of a religious nature. As there is a difference of nature between faith and reason, there is a difference too between moral convictions and religious beliefs, and consequently between 'moral objection' and 'religious objection' depending on whether the objection obeys prescriptions dictated by morality or by religion (cult-related prescriptions). However, this distinction is not always perceptible by someone who has doubts about rationality or who does not clearly conceive the difference between faith and reason, between natural and supernatural orders.[162]

Two clarifications are useful at the outset:

— *About the rationality of religious beliefs:*

Any conviction or belief, even of a religious nature, is rational *stricto sensu*, because a conviction is a 'reasoned certitude', as elucidated in the first part of this study. So, a religious belief is partly produced by reason, since to achieve it, reason must first judge whether the religious principle is credible or not and deliberate in order to determine the way in which this principle is applied to

160 ECHR, *Evans v. United Kingdom*, n° 6339/05, 10 April 2007, § 71; *Pretty v. United Kingdom*, § 61.

161 ECHR, *Christine Goodwin v. United Kingdom*, GC, n° 28957/95, 1 December 1997, § 90.

162 Faith and reason are two modes of knowledge of a same reality; their contradictions are therefore symptoms of error or ignorance.

individual cases, then submit its conclusion to the judgment of conscience. If conscience adopts this conclusion, the latter becomes a religious conviction.

As to the moral conviction, it can fully be considered rational (and called '*dictamen rationis*'), because it results from the application by reason, to individual cases, of the basic moral standard ("*doing good and avoiding evil*"), which—contrary to religious standards—is supposed to be conform to reason, since it is known evidently and universally.

— *About the uniqueness of conscience:*
Conscience passes its judgments through reason in the light of the information available to every individual. If the reason is not 'right', i.e. if it 'reasons awry', or if it is not enlightened enough (as when the information available to the person is wrong or insufficient), conscience cannot pass good judgments. Now, even though conscience is informed by data both profane and religious in nature, it would be excessive to distinguish between a *prescription of conscience* and a *religious prescription*,[163] between a religious conscience and a moral conscience. Indeed, as there is only one conscience in every person, any conviction, whether moral (profane) or religious, is always the product of a unique conscience, which dictates what should and should not be done. This uniqueness of conscience does not however prevent the possibility of making a distinction between moral prescription and religious prescription, and, consequently, between moral objection and religious objection.

a The Distinction between Moral Objection and Religious Objection

i *Moral Objection*

Moral objection (which is rational *stricto sensu*) is motivated by a prescription based on reason, a *'dictamen rationis'*, excluding any religious or cult-related prescription. It is the consequence of a judgment by conscience upon the very nature of the act objected to, in the light of the basic moral standard (doing good, avoiding evil) from which originates the innate sense of justice. The objection is about an objectively knowable situation to which the subject applies this basic moral standard: it results from a moral judgment.

Such a moral objection, directed against acts contrary to basic moral standards (not to kill, not to harm, not to steal, not to lie, not to affect others' dignity, etc.) is independent of religion. It does not aim at opposing a religious prescription which seeks to accomplish an act. More importantly, it calls into question the very morality (and justice) of the act objected to: the individual

163 As I did in an article published in *La Nef*, n° 232, December 2011: *"Objecter au nom de la justice"* (objection in the name of justice).

is convinced that it would be evil and unfair to accomplish such an act. This moral objection manifests the exteriority (the transcendence) of individual conscience vis-à-vis the positive law, as well as the imperative link which relates it to the sense of justice, since from the moral objection originates from the latter. The ECtHR itself recognised the existence of a difference between morality and positive law, since in a recent case it censored the restriction imposed on the freedom of expression of an opponent to abortion, explaining that the opponent's discourse could be perceived *"as a way of creating awareness of the more general fact that law may diverge from morality"*.[164]

ii Religious Objection

Religious objection, for its part, results from a religious or cult-related prescription, the acceptance of which by an individual's conscience necessitates an act of faith and does not impose itself on reason. It is an objection indicating the objector's religion and having a direct, necessary and sufficient link with it. Religions abound in material prescriptions aimed at guiding, in the most concrete aspects, the daily life of the faithful. We might mention the prohibition against eating meat on Friday, touching pork, working on certain days of the week, receiving a blood transfusion or showing one's face among many others.[165] The fact that some of these religious prescriptions, considered individually, may be questionable is irrelevant,[166] since they can be rational with respect to the paradigms underlying them. But—and here lies the big difference with moral objection—a religious (or cult-related) objection does not directly question the justice of the act objected to, since the latter is perceived as unjust in an indirect way only from the point of view of faith. The objector cannot claim that this act, considered in isolation and independently of faith, would be unjust *in itself*. As an example, if a Mormon were to judge in conscience that he should refuse to drink tea in order to comply with the precepts of his religion, he cannot claim that drinking tea is in itself immoral or unjust, unless the objective health danger of this product could be established (which would then confer a moral nature upon his objection).

---

164 ECHR, *Annen v. Germany*, n° 3690/10, 26 November 2015, § 63. In so doing, the Court followed the observations submitted to it by the *European Centre for Law and Justice*.

165 In the Jewish religion, the 613 mitzvot (commandments) regulate those aspects of daily life.

166 See, for instance, ECHR, *Skugar and others v. Russia*, n° 40010/04, 3 December 2009, concerning the attribution of a taxpayer number for the payment of taxes, which would mean, according to the applicants, their "marking by the Beast" and their alienation from the Orthodox Church.

The Bible gives numerous examples of such conscientious objections of a religious nature. For instance, in the second book of the Maccabees, the refusal by seven brothers and their mother to eat *"swine's flesh against the law"*[167] led them to martyrdom. Each of the brothers, under torture and faced with the executioner, declared *"I will not obey the commandment of the king, but the commandment of the law, which was given to us by Moses"*. A few decades after, before the Sanhedrin which ordered them not to evangelize any more, Peter and the Apostles gave virtually the same answer: *"We must obey God rather than human beings."*[168]

iii *Mixed Objections*

Finally, the objection can be mixed, since certain prescriptions are both religious and moral, for instance the negative precepts of Decalogue (do not kill, do not steal, do not lie, etc.).[169] Given that there exists, *in fine*, only one justice and that our conscience is informed both by religious and profane data, it is often difficult to establish whether the objection is of a moral or religious nature. Thus, some individuals invoke only their religious beliefs to justify an objection which is however of a mainly moral nature.[170] So a person will oppose abortion in the name of his religion, whereas a reference to the moral principle which prohibits harm would be sufficient. Such an approach not only adds to the confusion of the concept of conscientious objection, but it weakens the objection in question by tainting its relation to justice with the suspicion of irrationality often attached to religion.

Such a mixed objection can be found in the Biblical story of Schiphra and Pua, the Hebrew midwives[171] who refused to execute the unjust order of Pharaoh to kill all male Hebrew new-borns: *"But the midwives feared God and did not do as the king of Egypt commanded them, but let the male children live."* (Ex. 1, 17). The motive of their behaviour is explicitly given by the Bible: *"But the midwives feared God…"*, referring to God's justice.[172] From the Biblical point of view, all moral objections are religious too, because the Judeo-Christian faith teaches that God engraved his eternal law in the hearts of men: thus human

---

167 2 Maccabees 7, 1–41.

168 *Acts of the Apostles*, 5, 29.

169 Being the moral bedrock of human action, indeed largely translated in human rights, these prescriptions certainly offer a legitimate foundation for conscientious objection.

170 ECHR, *Eweida and others v. UK*.

171 In the first chapter of the book of Exodus (Ex. 1, 15–21).

172 Jacques Suaudeau, *L'objection de conscience ou le devoir de désobéir: Ses origines et son application dans le domaine de la santé*, Peuple libre, 2013.

conscience is the *"voice of God"*[173] which raised man to spiritual life—it is the *"seat of God in the soul"*.[174] Hence acting against conscience equates to *"acting against God"*.[175]

In any case, although an objection, whether rational (moral) or religious, always constitutes a conscientious objection, the difference between moral objection and religious objection lies in the fact that the former can pretend to be objectively just: its claim has to do with *justice*. It should be possible to raise a just objection by full right, and it should not be feasible to legitimately oppose it through a sanction or constraint. Conversely, a religious (or cult-related) objection cannot pretend to be just in itself, and its claim has then to do with *freedom* of the individual to comply with the judgment of his conscience as to the application in his case of his religion's prescriptions. In consequence, the recognition of a religious objection by public authorities may depend on particular circumstances, especially on their will to respect religious freedom and to tolerate religious minorities.

b How to Recognize a Moral Objection (Based on Justice)

The non-religiosity of an objection is insufficient as a guarantee of its objective justice. Besides, it could seem impossible to determine whether an objection is truly moral (and therefore just) in a society which has given up, in the name of relativism and subjectivism, the conviction that there exists such a thing as an objective good. But refusing to accomplish this would amount to relinquishing the rationality of justice and resigning oneself to the arbitrary.

Four criteria can be identified to determine whether an objection is of a moral nature and, consequently, whether it is based on a requirement of justice.

i *The Moral Objection should Aim to Respect what is Just and Good*

In order to be "moral", the objection should aim at justice and/or good; hence it should oppose an attack against a fundamental right (for instance, the right to life or physical integrity) or against an objective good (for instance, the natural environment). Any objection not aiming at respect for a fundamental right or of good would not be moral.

---

173 Saint Ambrose, *De paradisio*, 14, 69, *PL*, 14, 309; Saint Augustine, *De sermone Domini in Monte*, 2, 9, 32, *PL*, 34 1283, p. 297; God speaks to everyone *"by the voice of conscience"*.

174 Saint Augustine, *Enarrationes in* PS 45, 9, *PL*, 25, 22B: *"God has his throne in the conscience of the just"*.

175 Saint Thomas Aquinas, *Super Epistolam ad Galatas*, 5.1 n° 282: "*... the conviction that something must be done is nothing else but a judgment that it would be against God's will not to do it*".

ii *The Commandment Objected to Derogates from a Right or a Basic Principle*

This second criterion correlates with the first, because the reason why the objection aims at respect for what is just or good is that the commandment infringes it. Though legal, this commandment creates an exception or a derogation to a principle. The existence of such an exception can often be observed in positive law or in the history of the norm, the application of which is refused. For instance, abortion was conceived as an exception to the principle of respect for human life, and the same goes for destructive research on the embryo. Euthanasia and war[176] are derogations or justificatory facts in the face of prohibitions against homicide. Similarly, the authorization of corrida can be understood to derogate from the rules governing the slaughter of animals. In fact, when the order objected to derogates from a right or a basic principle, it aims at an action which is authorized by law but that nobody could freely accomplish in the absence of such authorization (no individual is free to practice abortion or euthanasia on his own authority or to declare war).

The French permanent dictionary of bioethics and biotechnologies describes in this way the field of application of conscientious objection in the medical sphere: it *"concerns all medical non-therapeutic acts, when they carry the seeds of a risk to harm the integrity or dignity of the individual or to reify the human person."*[177] Indeed, for a medical act to be licit—and to be medical *stricto sensu*—it must be therapeutic, and respect the principles of the dignity and primacy of the human being,[178] and of integrity and unavailability of the human body. The laws allowing abortion,[179] contraceptive sterilisation,[180] or scientific research on the person (including the embryo) without personal benefit have instituted derogations from those principles. In fact, the legislator which permits derogation from such principles often accompanies such

176 Though war is not necessarily an injustice, it is however an evil.

177 *Dictionnaire permanent. Bioéthique et biotechnologies*, Éditions législatives.

178 Convention on Human Rights and Biomedicine, Article 2—Primacy of the human being "The interests and welfare of the human being shall prevail over the sole interest of society or science."

179 Both by chirurgical and drug treatment.

180 In France, contraceptive sterilisation, qualified by the Court of Cassation as an infringement of the integrity of the human body and prohibited by Article 16–3 of the Civil Code (in an opinion of 6 July 1998, Juris-Data n° 1998–003278), is henceforward made licit by the legislator (L. n° 2001–588, 4 July 2001: JCP G 2001, III, 20528). The conscience clause for doctors is extended to contraceptive sterilisation. Christian BYK, *BIOÉTHIQUE.—Législation, jurisprudence et avis des instances d'éthique*, JCP G. n° 26, 26 June 2002, I 146.

derogation with a conscience clause.[181] Therefore, if the legislator institutes a conscience clause while decriminalizing abortion, that legislator does not do it out of respect for the diversity of individual opinions concerning abortion, but so that no one would be obliged to participate in an objective evil which is alien to the normal practice of medicine, albeit necessary from his point of view. In so doing, the legislator recognizes the moral imperfection of his laws and restricts their compelling character, because compelling medical professionals to take a *personal* part in a violation of these principles would be contrary to justice, even if the society *collectively* deems such derogation necessary. This explains too why no one can be compelled, in the United States, to take part in a capital execution.[182]

This criterion related to derogation from a right or a basic principle underlies the possible conflict between the collective level, from which the commandment derives its authority, and the individual level at which the said commandment must be executed. The obedience of the individual to the community does not raise any difficulty when the common or collective good is realised through a particular good. But a problem does arise when the community considers that some particular evils are necessary or should be tolerated, in view of a lesser evil or even good, for instance respect for individual freedom (abortion) or the advancement of scientific knowledge (research on the human being), or because the legalization of a practice would represent the most efficient way of circumscribing it (prostitution, surrogate motherhood, drugs).

The toleration or legalisation of an evil by political authorities is one thing, and compelling an individual to take a personal part in the realisation of this evil is another. This is because political authorities consider the end, while the individual is confronted with the means. These are two opposing aspects of morality: the first takes into account a general intention (the end), and the other has to deal with the object of the action (the means). Now, one cannot act from the perspective of the end alone, disregarding the material action. This is the reason why, when the State tolerates evils that it deems necessary or inevitable, it is only fair that their realisation be its exclusive duty, and that it should use means which do not compel anyone.

---

181 Article L. 2212–8 CSP: "A doctor is never obliged to practice [...] No midwife, no nurse or male nurse, no paramedic, whoever he is, is obliged to participate in an interruption of pregnancy."

182 18 U.S.C. § 3597 (b). *Excuse of an employee on moral or religious grounds*, See Nadia N. Sawicki, *Doctors, Discipline, and the Death Penalty: Professional Implications of Safe Harbor*, Yale Law & Policy Review Fall, 2008.

Such a problematic situation is encountered more and more in liberal society, which is characterized by a differentiation between public morality and private morality and by the greater part recognized to individual freedom, the individual being left free to use controversial practices. So, according to this societal model, the individual, while tolerating a practice used in social and political life—such as abortion, euthanasia or prostitution (because he considers it illegitimate to oppose the will of others)—will be able to strongly object being associated with them in a personal capacity. The freedom that liberal society grants to individuals in these "moral" matters can only be fair if it permits both those who adhere to these practices and those who oppose them to live according to their beliefs.

iii *The Objection is Universalizable*

Kant's categorical imperative offers an additional criterion of rationality and justice: *"Act only according to that* maxim whereby you can, at the same time, will that it should become a universal law."[183] One must then wonder if society could continue to function in the event that none of its members agrees to perform the act objected to. More concretely, would a society be viable in the absence of old age insurance,[184] vaccine, nuclear energy, same-sex unions, adoption by same-sex pairs?

This criterion of 'universalizability' of the objection overlaps the criterion of respect for others' rights, except that it is more satisfactory. Indeed, the multiplication of subjective rights, more or less related to a fundamental right, leads to the following: respect for others' rights does not really appear as a satisfying criterion for judging an objection. The recognition of a positive "right" to abortion or euthanasia cannot make conscientious objection irrational in these matters. The fact that an objection affects the rights of others, as recognised by a positive law or a judgement, is not sufficient to make this objection unjust if and when subjective rights can themselves be detached from justice. For instance, the rights to a child (by IVF or adoption), abortion or euthanasia are not in themselves required by justice (which is always relational), but express a will to respect personal autonomy (which is one-sided).

In fine, we may note that this criterion of 'universalizability' of the objection is directed toward the common good. A non-universalizable objection will be

183 Emmanuel Kant, *Grounding for the Metaphysics of Morals*, in *The* Metaphysics *of Morals*, I, *Foundation, Introduction.*

184 European Commission on Human Rights, *V. v. Netherlands*, n° 10678/83, dec., 5 July 1984.

aimed at a particular good, and, therefore, it will not express a rational moral conviction focused on justice.

iv The Objection is about an Ethically Sensitive Question

Given that morality is rapidly mutating in present-day society, it is difficult to judge the rationality of an objection in some fields where consensus on a matter no longer exists. With regard to such highly debated subjects, the Parliamentary Assembly of the Council of Europe makes a useful point when it calls the Member States to *"ensure the right to well-defined conscientious objection in relation to morally sensitive matters, such as military service or other services related to health care and education…"*.[185] The Assembly has largely in mind bioethics and religious or sexual education. Its recommendation is a wise one: society may not agree about what is good, but it is obvious that some questions are debatable because of their high ethical sensitiveness. This is a useful empirical criterion.

5 *Distance between the Object and Motive of the Objection*

In order to judge an objection, one must also take into account the distance between its object (the act) and its motive (the conviction). Being forced to hold a rifle is not the same as being forced to use it. Doing the housework in an abortion clinic is not the same as performing an abortion. Any act commits the conscience of its actor in varying degrees according to circumstances that need to be evaluated case by case. The ECtHR clearly expresses the necessity of a sufficiently close relationship between the object and the cause of the objection: *"Even where the belief in question attains the required level of cogency and importance, it cannot be said that every act which is in some way inspired, motivated or influenced by it constitutes a "manifestation" of the belief. Thus, for example, acts or omissions which do not directly express the belief concerned or which are only remotely connected to a precept of faith fall outside the protection of Article 9 § 1"*.[186]

The ECtHR specifies that *"the existence of a sufficiently close and direct nexus between the act and the underlying belief must be determined on the facts of each*

185 PACE, Resolution 1928 (2013) of 24 April 2013, *Safeguarding human rights in relation to religion and belief, and protecting religious communities from violence*, art. 9.10.

186 ECHR, *Eweida and others v. UK*, § 82. See also *Skugar and others v. Russia* and, for instance, *Arrowsmith v. United Kingdom*, n° 7050/75, Commission report of 12 October 1978, (DR) 19, p. 5, *C. v. United Kingdom*, n° 10358/83, Commission report of 15 December 1983, DR 37, p. 142, and ECHR, *Zaoui v. Switzerland*, dec., n° 41615/98, 18 January 2001.

case."[187] Thus, for the objection to be serious, there must exist a sufficiently *'close and direct'* nexus between the motive and the object of the objection,[188] so that the person will be morally committed by the action. If the objector is ordered personally to perform the act objected to (for example an obstetrician ordered to perform an abortion), he is morally committed, and the question of distance is irrelevant. On the other hand, if he does not perform the reproved act, but plays some part in the procedure (e.g. by indicating the name of a doctor who might perform the abortion), the said distance must be evaluated, and this should be done by using criteria—classical in moral philosophy—which make a distinction as to whether the cooperation is direct or indirect, formal or material, near or distant.

a The Need for a Direct Nexus, and the Doctrine of the Double Effect

The existence of a "direct nexus" means that the individual would be made, if he were to perform the act causing his objection, to directly collaborate in the evil reproved by his conscience: *"This collaboration is called direct when there can be no doubt as to the determined intention of the main actor."*[189] Thus, a pharmacist is morally committed in a direct way when he sells an abortive product to a female customer, since this product does not leave any doubt concerning its future use and effects. Such is not the case with contraceptive methods, which can be prescribed for a purpose other than contraception. Likewise, in normal circumstances, an arms dealer is not directly committed by the use of the arms he sells insofar as they can be used for a good cause, such as self-defence.

The need for a direct nexus between the motive and the object of the objection allows us to take into account situations which raise the problem of the "double effect",[190] namely situations in which the same act produces both good and bad effects. Can somebody object to an act because it can produce evil? The answer, classical in moral philosophy,[191] consists in verifying firstly that the good effect is the sole intention of the act, secondly that the bad effect is not desired in itself, thirdly that the good effect results from the act, not from the bad effect, and fourthly that the bad effect is not disproportionate to the good effect.

---

187 ECHR, *Eweida and others v. UK*, § 82.

188 European Commission on Human Rights, *Borre Arnold Knudsen v. Norway*, dec., n° 11045/84, 8 March 1985.

189 Jacques Suaudeau, *L'objection de conscience. Son application dans le domaine de la santé.*

190 Also labelled "indirect voluntary" act.

191 St. Thomas Aquinas, *Summa Theologica*, II–II, Qu. 64, Art. 7.

An idea which derives from this doctrine is that an evil can be tolerated only as the price to be paid for a good at least equal to it, and provided that this sought good does not result from the said evil. This last condition according to which the evil should only be a side effect of the action, not a means to attain the sought good, complies with the moral rule that an evil cannot produce a good, otherwise the aim would justify the means.

According to this theory of the double effect, a doctor who objects in principle to abortion would not in conscience be prevented from prescribing (and would even be compelled to prescribe) for a pregnant woman whose life is in danger a treatment liable to provoke an abortion as a side effect. In such a case, the treatment does not aim at an abortion, but at saving the life of the woman, and the value of the woman's life is proportionate to the value of the unborn child. The nexus between the act and its reproved effect is then indirect. In a case like this, the doctor cannot object without breaching his duty of care. It is different when a woman expresses the desire to abort for personal reasons, such as her economic situation: in this case, the good effect sought (limitation of expenditure) is not proportionate to the value of the sacrificed life and results of the bad effect itself.

b The Need for a Close Nexus

The required collaboration in the reproved act must also be sufficiently close or near for the objection to be justified. However, since the objector's collaboration, even distant, is necessary for the performance of the reproved act, it is as morally committing as a near collaboration, and the objection is then justified from this point of view. Such is the case, for instance, not only of the prescription, sale and administration of an abortion pill, but also of its manufacture. Similarly, if an objecting doctor indicates to a woman the address of one of his colleagues who practices abortion, he is morally committed, since the mere information he gives will contribute to the performance of an abortion. In the same way also, a pharmacist who sells the abortion pill is not less committed than the nurse who administers it or the doctor who performs a surgical abortion: the abortion method is irrelevant. The same goes for a person who assists in a suicide by preparing the poison.

The ECtHR takes into account the need for this close nexus. For example, it considered that this condition is not fulfilled when the refusal to pay taxes is motivated only by opposition to abortion,[192] or to the army,[193] or when

192 European Commission on Human Rights, *Bouessel du Bourg v. France*, n° 2074/92, dec., 18 February 1993.

193 European Commission on Human Rights, *C. v. UK*, n° 10358/83, dec., 15 December 1983. See also HRC, *JP v. Canada*, Communication n° 446/1991.

opposition to abortion is invoked by a pastor to justify his refusal to exercise the functions of registrar incumbent on him.[194] Similarly, the former European Commission on Human Rights considered that a tax-payer cannot object to the payment of his taxes simply because the State finances a religion he does not adhere to.[195] This is also the position of the Human Rights Committee, which declared inadmissible the complaint of a person who refused to pay a percentage of her taxes corresponding to the portion of the Canadian federal budget dedicated to military expenditure.[196]

When the distance between the object and the cause of the objection is too great to justify a really personal conscientious objection, the corresponding refusal can be connected to the concept of civil disobedience. Such was the case, for instance, of Henry David Thoreau, arrested and imprisoned in 1846 for refusing to pay the head tax to Massachusetts because he accused this State of being an accomplice to slavery and war in Mexico. As to the practice of *boycott*, it is another distant form of objection by which a person abstains from doing something which it is not compulsory for him to do, in order to avoid contributing, even in a distant way, to the interests of a person or a group whose action he morally reproves.

6 *The Question of the Relationship with Nature*

The relationship with nature is less a criterion than a question closely bound from now on to the theme of conscientious objection. In fact, until the recent technological and industrial revolutions, conscientious objection was primarily motivated by personal interrelationships, for only such interrelationships could bring justice into the equation. Now, the emergence of new technologies capable of deeply changing nature has given birth to new motives of objection, which are no more based on respect for human rights, but on the preservation of nature and environment, as well as on safeguarding living conditions for future generations. Thus, the extension of the power available to man had the correlative effect of enlarging both his responsibilities and his moral obligations. However, because there is no exact definition of 'nature', including

194 ECHR, *Borre Arnold Knudsen v. Norway.*

195 ECHR, *Darby v. Sweden*, n° 11581/85, 9 May 1989; *Iglesia Bautista "El Salvador" and José Aquilino Ortega Moratilla v. Spain*, n° 17522/90, 22 December 1992.

196 HRC, *Dr. J.P. v. Canada*, par. 4.2. The Committee noted that "[*a*]*lthough article 18 of the Covenant certainly protects the right to hold, express and disseminate opinions and convictions, including conscientious objection to military activities and expenditures, the refusal to pay taxes on grounds of conscientious objection clearly falls outside the scope of protection of this article*".

'human nature', it remains to be seen whether a reference to nature can valuably justify objecting to practices like human cloning, hybridisation man/animal/machine or, topically, adoption of children by same-sex partners,[197] eugenics or surrogate motherhood.

If one is aware of the fact that nature determines human life, one may admit that its respect can be a legitimate and rational motive for objection. Such an objection expresses a belief relating both to nature and the extent of man's freedom towards it. Thus, this is not a question of justice between persons, but a question of rightness of man's action in his environment, i.e. "prudence", in other words, a question of natural law.

This question is all the more delicate since the very identification of what is natural, objective and hence pre-moral, or amoral, is at stake through the relationship with nature. Indeed, this relationship remains pre-moral, or amoral as long as only the *direct perception* of nature by man is at stake. On the other hand, it acquires a moral dimension when the human doing is solicited. For instance, though the belief that the earth is at the centre of the universe does not have, in principle, any moral connotation, if this belief derives from a *factual* error as opposed to a *moral* error (it is morally irrelevant that the earth is or is not at the centre of the universe), such a belief will nevertheless affect the conception of the world, and therefore the moral judgment of those who hold it. Similarly, any conception of human nature—be it pre-moral or amoral—necessarily has an impact on the moral judgment made about what is licit or illicit as it affects man. For instance, though Western people now largely accept homosexuality and, consequently, favour the extension of marriage and adoption of children to same-sex partners, such an acceptance results less from a

197 In *Eweida and others v. UK*, the applicants relied exclusively on their religious beliefs, not on freedom of conscience, to justify their refusal. While sustaining that their refusal was a manifestation of their religious beliefs, they invited the Court to judge from the standpoint of Article 9, paragraph 2 of the Convention, which allows the balancing of competing interests. Yet, the objection to civil marriage between same-sex persons does not necessarily result from religious beliefs and can be made by an atheist. Objectors can refer to the natural definition of marriage—such is reflected, among other places, in Article 12 of the Convention—as being the union of a nubile man and a nubile woman in order to start a family, the latter being *"the natural and fundamental element of society and [having] a right to by protected by both society and the State"* (DUDH, art. 16). This right was already considered as a natural right when the European Convention was written (Collected Edition of the "Travaux Préparatoires" of the European Convention of Human Rights, vol. II, Martinus Nijhoff, The Hague, 1975, Consultative Assembly, first session, 8 September 1949). This definition of marriage, adopted in international law, is shared by certain religions but does not depend on them.

general movement towards tolerance[198] than from the belief that homosexuality is natural. Thus, this acceptance therefore results from a change of the pre-moral perception of nature in this regard.

When the objection is about school teaching, a reflection on the relationship of this objection with nature (or science) is also necessary. It is indeed a well-known fact that religions, philosophies and sciences offer conceptions of the world and nature which may sometimes turn out to be mutually incompatible. Thus, the theory of evolution and the story of the creation of the universe, found in the book of Genesis, radically oppose each other at first sight. Now, since knowledge is necessary to exercise a judgement in conscience, the religious objection of some parents to the teaching of scientific theories to their children should be regarded as illegitimate if those parents deny, on principle, any value to scientific knowledge. In contrast, this objection becomes legitimate if the teaching goes beyond what can be legitimately guaranteed by science.

Similarly, it is not uncommon that compulsory sex education,[199] lessons in secular morality,[200] and lessons in ethics,[201] spark the objection of parents, since these questions are closely related to morality and religion. Until now, the ECtHR systematically denied parents the right to object in these matters, considering that, as to these, the education was provided in an objective, pluralistic and scientific manner and was not an attempt at indoctrination.[202] Again, the criterion of justice is the determination of what is objective, pluralistic and scientific: personal beliefs cannot prevail over what is earnestly held as scientific.

The ECtHR has held that the education must be *"given in an objective, critical and pluralistic manner"* and that because of the respect due to parents *"[t]he State is forbidden to pursue an aim of indoctrination that might be considered as not respecting parents' religious and philosophical convictions."*[203] If this limit is exceeded, the parents' objection is then legitimate and can be founded on

198 The growing intolerance towards people hostile to homosexuality would rather be proof to the contrary.

199 ECHR, *Jiménez Alonso et Jiménez Merino v. Spain*, n° 51188/99, dec., 25 May 2000; *Kjeldsen, Busk, Madsen and Pedersen v. Denmark*, n° 5095/71…, 7 December 1976, § 54; *Dojan and others v. Germany*, n° 319/08, dec., 13 December 2011.

200 European Commission on Human Rights, *Sluijs v. Belgium*, n° 17568/90, dec., 9 September 1992.

201 ECHR, *Appel-Irrgang v. Germany*, n° 45216/07, dec., 6 October 2009.

202 Moreover, the Court noted that parents retain the possibility of educating their children and of choosing another school more in keeping with their beliefs.

203 ECHR, *Folgerø and others v. Norway*, § 84(h); *Kjeldsen and others v. Denmark*, § 53.

Article 2, second sentence, of Protocol n° 1, according to which: *"In the exercise of any functions which it assumes in relation to education and to teaching, the State shall respect the right of parents to ensure such education and teaching in conformity with their own religious and philosophical convictions."* The Court stipulated that *"[i]t enjoins the State to respect parents' convictions, be they religious or philosophical, throughout the entire State education programme"* and, this *"duty is broad in its extent".*[204]

Such difference between convictions and beliefs and scientific 'knowledge' predetermines the difference between education and instruction. The ECtHR defined the *"education of children"* as being *"the whole process whereby, in any society, adults endeavour to transmit their beliefs, culture and other values to the young, whereas teaching or instruction refers in particular to the transmission of knowledge and to intellectual development."*[205]

Thus, by the mere claim that teaching is scientific, or that a practice is natural, public authorities will be able to make any moral or religious objection against them inoperative. One can see the danger of Lysenkoism, which exists both in the scientific and the social field, re-emerging here. For a State, this attitude consists in pretending to peremptorily define science and nature and in repressing those who do not share its point of view. A liberal State should then refrain from expressing itself about what is 'natural' or 'scientific' beyond what is commonly admitted as such. The State is liable to open itself to the contradictory judgment of persons when it does so, for instance when it claims that an eight-month foetus is not a human being or that a child can have two fathers or two mothers.

IV Rights and Obligations of the State

The criteria of evaluation defined above allow a judgment to be made as to whether a said objection expresses a personal preference or instead derives from a religious belief or a moral conviction. The obligations of the State, in this regard, vary depending on whether this objection pertains to the first or second hypothesis.

1 *Faced with a "Personal Convenience"*

A belief which is neither religious (nor philosophical) nor moral must be regarded as a simple *personal convenience* or preference which does not deserve

204 ECHR, *Folgerø and others v. Norway*, § 84; see also *Kjeldsen and others v. Denmark*, § 51.

205 ECHR, *Campbell and Cosans v. United Kingdom*, § 33.

protection under Article 9 of the ECHR. The judge might however estimate that certain preferences or choices come within the scope of other rights, such as the right to respect for personal autonomy,[206] such right being itself guaranteed under the right to respect for private life provided for in Article 8 of the ECHR. This is the case, especially, with regard to personal and relational choices and desires, linked—among others—to *'physical'*[207] and *'psychological'*[208] integrity, *'personal fulfilment'*,[209] *'personal development'*,[210] *'identity'*,[211] *'sexual identity'*[212] and the desire to have children[213] or to die.[214]

2 *Faced with a Moral Conviction or a Religious Belief*

The respect due to the objection varies considerably depending on whether it is based on a moral conviction or a religious belief: respect for the objection is a *right* in the first case and *toleration* in the second case, since the aforementioned respect concerns the objection in the first case and the objector in the second.

a Faced with a Moral Conviction

i *The Objector cannot be Coerced nor Sanctioned*

Insofar as a moral conviction is founded in justice, it deserves to be recognised as a right, and the conscientious objector cannot be coerced or sanctioned. Sanctioning would amount to denying his personal responsibility in the face of the order (that is to say, blaming him for not being an automaton to the State) and would imply that the acts in question (war, abortion, euthanasia, etc.) are good things in themselves: the moral rationale would then be overturned.

This is why the Human Rights Committee judged that *"repression of the refusal to be drafted for compulsory military service, exercised against persons whose conscience or religion prohibits the use of arms, is incompatible with*

206 ECHR, *Pretty v. UK*, § 61.

207 *X and Y v. Netherlands*, n° 8978/80, 26 March 1985, § 22; ECHR, *Salvetti v. Italy*, n° 42197/98, 9 July 2002.

208 ECHR, *Solomakhin v. Ukraine*, n° 24429/03, 15 March 2012, § 33.

209 ECHR, *K.A. and A.D. v. Belgium v. UK*, n° 42758/98 and 45558/99, 17 February 2005, § 83.

210 ECHR, *Christine Goodwin*, § 90.

211 ECHR, *Mikulić v. Croatia*, n° 53173/99, 7 February 2002, § 34; see also *Jäggi v. Switzerland*, n° 58757/00, 13 July 2006, § 37.

212 ECHR, *Y.Y. v. Turkey*, 10 March 2015, n° 14793/08. This was about the right to choose one's sex.

213 ECHR, *Costa and Pavan v. Italy; Evans v. United Kingdom*, n° 6339/50, 10 April 2007; *Dickson v. United Kingdom*, n° 44362/04, 4 December 2007.

214 ECHR, *Haas v. Switzerland*, n° 31322/07, 20 January 2011, § 51.

article 18, paragraph 1, of the Covenant",[215] which guarantees freedom of conscience and religion. Confronted with a conscientious objection to military service, the State should not punish objectors; at most, *"A State party may, if it wishes, compel the objector to undertake a civilian alternative to military service, outside of the military sphere and not under military command. The alternative service must not be of a punitive nature, but must rather be a real service to the community and compatible with respect for human rights."*[216]

It may be concluded, by analogy, that when a health worker refuses to perform an abortion or euthanasia, he cannot be compelled to do so, and his refusal cannot be met with any penalty. The objector may however be required to carry out, in the interest of fairness, other useful tasks compatible with his conviction and respect for human rights.

ii *It is Incumbent upon the State to Positively Guarantee Respect for this Right by Taking Reasonable and Appropriate Measures*

As stated by Judges Vučinić and De Gaetano, of the ECHR, *"once that a genuine and serious case of conscientious objection is established, the State is obliged to respect the individual's freedom of conscience both positively (by taking reasonable and appropriate measures to protect the rights of the conscientious objector) and negatively (by refraining from actions which punish the objector or discriminate against him or her.)"*[217]

When confronted with applications lodged by persons and organisations complaining about difficulties to access legal abortion because of the great number of objectors in Poland and Italy, the institutions of both the United Nations and the Council of Europe never considered confining the right to conscientious objection to abortion. Thus, concerning Poland, the ECtHR noted *"that Polish law has acknowledged the need to ensure that doctors are not obliged to carry out services to which they object, and put in place a mechanism by which such a refusal can be expressed"*; it then concluded that *"[t]his mechanism also includes elements allowing the right to conscientious objection to be reconciled with the patient's interests."*[218] The ECtHR limited itself to obliging the State,

215 HRC, *Cenk Atasoy and Arda Sarkut v. Turkey*, 2012, § 10.5. See also HRC, *Jeong and others v. Republic of Korea*, 2011.

216 HRC, *Jong-nam Kim and others v. Republic of Korea*, 2012, § 7.4. See also HRC, *Atasoy and Sarkut v. Turkey*, 2012, § 10.4. Underlined by us.

217 ECHR, *Eweida and others v. UK*, partly dissenting joint opinion of Judges Vučinić and De Gaetano, § 3.

218 ECHR, *P. and S. v. Poland*, n° 57375/08, 30 October 2012, § 107, unofficial translation. See also ECHR, *R.R. v. Poland*, n° 27617/08, 26 May 2011, § 206.

since abortion is legal in Poland, to ensure that *"the legal framework devised for this purpose [is] shaped in a coherent manner which allows the different legitimate interests involved to be taken into account adequately and in accordance with the obligations deriving from the Convention."*[219] In other words, the Court reminded the State of its responsibility, when it decides to legalise abortion, to create a mechanism which guarantees access to this practice while respecting the right to conscientious objection.

The same approach was adopted by the Human Rights Committee,[220] and the Special Rapporteur of the United Nations *"on the right of everyone to the enjoyment of the highest attainable standard of physical and mental health"*.[221] These bodies considered that public authorities should not weigh the right to conscientious objection against the "right" to abortion, but that they should reconcile the exercise of both rights in order to guarantee them. This is also the position of Heiner Bielefedt, the UN Special Rapporteur on freedom of religion or belief,[222] who recognises a right to conscientious objection for medical staff.[223]

It should be noted however that access to legal abortion does not enjoy the same protection as the right to respect for freedom of conscience,[224] because it is not guaranteed by international instruments as a human right.[225]

As far as abortion is concerned, such an approach—by virtue of which the State has a positive obligation to take measures aiming to protect the conscientious objector's rights, as well as to reconcile, in some cases, contradictory rights and interests—has also been adopted by the European Committee of Social Rights (Council of Europe). In a complaint against Italy, the IPPF (International Planned Parenthood Federation) criticized *"… the failure of the competent authorities to adopt the necessary measures which are required to compensate for the deficiencies in service provision [abortion] caused by health personnel choosing to exercise their right of conscientious objection"*.[226] The

219 Especially ECHR, *R.R. v. Poland*, § 187; *P. and S. v. Poland*, § 99.

220 HRC, *V.D.A. v. Argentine*, Communication n° 1608/2007, 29 March 2011.

221 Report of Anand Grover on Poland, A/RHC/14/20. Ad. 3, § 85. See also his *amicus curiae* handed to the ECHR in the case *R.R. v. Poland*, in which he mentions *"the use of the conscientious objection clause by medical practitioners"*.

222 H. Bielefeldt et al., *Freedom of religion or belief, op. cit.*, pp. 298 and following.

223 H. Bielefeldt et al., *Freedom of religion or belief, op. cit.*, p. 301.

224 ECHR, *Chassagnou and others v. France*, GC, § 113.

225 G. Puppinck, "L'avortement et la CEDH", in *Mélanges en l'honneur de Gérard Mémeteau. Droit medical et éthique médicale: regards contemporains*, Les Études Hospitalières, 2015.

226 European Committee of Social Rights, *International Planned Parenthood Federation—European Network (IPPF EN) v. Italy*, n° 87/2012, 10 September 2013.

Committee reminded the State that it has an obligation to organise health services in order to reconcile respect for freedom of conscience exercisable by medical staff and access to abortion when it is legally performed.

b Faced with a Religious or Philosophical Belief

Objection resulting from a moral conviction is objectively founded, precisely by reason of the object opposed. By contrast, objection resulting from a religious or philosophical belief is not based on the *object* itself, but on the right to freedom of thought and religion of the *person* (i. α) and on the basis of the ideal of *democratic society* (i. ß), i.e. on a conception. In this regard, public authorities should aim at reconciling the rights and interests at stake (ii. α). However, since the objection cannot claim to be just in itself, its acceptance will be ultimately limited by the respect due to the fundamental values of society (ii. ß).

i *Foundation of Respect for a Person whose Objection is Based on a Religious Belief*

α Respect for the Objector as Part of Freedom of Conscience and Religion

A religious belief commands respect as part of freedom of conscience and religion. Public respect is not gained by the religious prescription itself, but by both the person's commitment to his conviction and his ability to conduct himself accordingly. This ability is peculiar to man and forms part of his ontological dignity. Such an approach to religious freedom was adopted by all major declarations of human rights of the second half of the twentieth century. It was also expressed by the Catholic Church during the second Vatican Council.[227]

Thus, respect for human dignity (in every man) implies a subjective (individual) right to concrete respect for its components, one of which is the spiritual dimension of human nature. This spiritual dimension especially takes the form of religious convictions. Freedom of religion is a unilateral subjective right originating in human nature; it is not inscribed in bilateral relations of justice, but tends to guarantee respect for the person himself. So, an infringement on religious freedom is more a violence than an injustice, because it tends to overstrain the link between the person and his belief. Society will respect this right as much as it wishes to respect "man" seen in an abstract way (ontological nature) and to avoid violence against (physical) persons. But given that

227 Declaration on religious freedom *Dignitatis Humanae*, on the right of the person and of communities to social and civil freedom in matters religious promulgated by His Holiness Pope Paul VI, 7 December 1965.

such subjective right is unilateral, it can upset and unbalance (multilateral) relations of justice within society; it can even upset society itself insofar as its present content is determined by everyone.

As respect for religious beliefs is based on human dignity, which is of an absolute nature, they command a respect considered as absolute by some, even if they always manifest themselves in a particular way. Though the State respects all beliefs *in abstracto*, it is confronted with their various peculiar manifestations *in concreto*. As it cannot recognise them as an absolute freedom or forbid them absolutely, its attitude toward them remains *tolerance* of a classical type. The fact remains that according to the approach to freedom of thought, conscience and religion based on human dignity, the right to respect for this freedom is not conceded, but only circumscribed by the State; it originates outside social life.

This right can also originate in social life, as part of the ideal of 'democratic society'.

β Respect for the Objector as Part of the Ideal of 'Democratic Society'

The cultural transformation of Western society modifies the foundation of freedom of conscience and religion. A new (collective) foundation emerges and tends to replace dignity (a personal one): it is the ideal of '*democratic society*'. However, since a person's conception of society controls his attitude toward conscientious objection, the source of the right to freedom of religion and conscience, which is absolute when it derives from man's dignity, becomes relative when it is based on the ideal of democratic society. This is because this ideal is less founded on ontology than on the desire to coexist, which is of an essentially practical nature. In any event, whether freedom is anchored in the ontological dignity of every human being or proceeds from tolerance, in both cases it takes the form of an undetermined subjective right whose exercise must be circumscribed by the State.

The ECtHR has developed its own doctrine regarding how concretely to take into account conscientious objection in the perspective of the ideal of a democratic society. According to the Court, a *"democratic society"* is characterized by *"pluralism, tolerance and broadmindedness"*.[228] Three concepts can summarize this doctrine: *pluralism, tolerance* and *compromise*. In practice, it is according to these three criteria that the Court judges if a sanction imposed on a person objecting for a religious or philosophical motive is justified.

228 ECHR, *Handyside v. United Kingdom*, n° 5493/72, 7 December 1976, § 49.

Pluralism

For the ECtHR, *"freedom of thought, conscience and religion is one of the foundations of a "democratic society" within the meaning of the Convention. It is, in its religious dimension, one of the most vital elements that go to make up the identity of believers and their conception of life, but it is also a precious asset for atheists, agnostics, sceptics and the unconcerned. The pluralism indissociable from a democratic society, which has been dearly won over the centuries, depends on it."*[229] According to the Court, there is no democracy without pluralism,[230] it is an '*indissociable*' link: democracy is characterized not only by pluralism, but also by *"the need to maintain true religious pluralism, which is vital to the survival of a democratic society."*[231] In line with this perspective, respect for religious pluralism aims not only at respecting persons, but also, and even primarily at the quality of the political regime. Pluralism sees diversity as a value in itself, which creates social conditions structurally favourable to the democratic regime.

Tolerance

The ECtHR states, pursuant to its conception of democracy, that the role of public authorities is not to avoid the causes of interreligious tensions by eliminating pluralism, but to favour tolerance between mutually opposed groups.[232] This means that tolerance is closely linked to safeguarding public order and religious peace.[233] Not only must different opinions and beliefs tolerate one another, but the State is equally obliged to tolerate those it might reprove. In fact, the role of the State is to be *"the neutral and impartial organiser of the exercise of various religions, faiths and beliefs"*. The Court considers that *"this role is conducive to public order, religious harmony and tolerance in a democratic society. The State's duty of neutrality and impartiality is incompatible with any power on the State's part to assess the legitimacy of religious beliefs or the ways in which those beliefs are expressed."*[234]

---

229 ECHR, *Kokkinakis v. Greece*, n° 14307/88, 25 May 1993, § 31; ECHR, *Buscarini and others v. San Marino*, GC, § 34.

230 ECHR, *United Communist Party of Turkey and others v. Turkey*, n° 19392/92, 30 January 1998, § 43.

231 ECHR, *Bayatyan v. Armenia*, § 122, citing *Manoussakis and others v. Greece*, § 44 and ECHR, *Metropolitan Church of Bessarabia and others v. Moldavia*, § 119.

232 ECHR, *United Communist Party of Turkey and others v. Turkey*, § 57 and ECHR, *Serif v. Greece*, n° 38178/97, 14 December 1999, § 53.

233 ECHR, *Bayatyan v. Armenia*, § 120.

234 *Idem.*

Compromise

Pluralism and tolerance require that the majority accepts to compromise so that democracy does not become a '*dictatorship of the majority*', since not only democracy is underlined by particular legal principles (Rule of Law) and philosophical principles (Human Rights), but moreover, it must not oppress its minority groups. The ECtHR postulated that "[*a*]*lthough individual interests must on occasion be subordinated to those of a group, democracy does not simply mean that the views of a majority must always prevail: a balance must be achieved which ensures the fair and proper treatment of people from minorities and avoids any abuse of a dominant position.*"[235] The Court added that "*Pluralism and democracy must also be based on dialogue and a spirit of compromise necessarily entailing various concessions on the part of individuals or groups of individuals which are justified in order to maintain and promote the ideals and values of a democratic society. Where these "rights and freedoms" are themselves among those guaranteed by the Convention or its Protocols, it must be accepted that the need to protect them may lead States to restrict other rights or freedoms likewise set forth in the Convention. It is precisely this constant search for a balance between the fundamental rights of each individual which constitutes the foundation of a 'democratic society'.*"[236]

The concrete form of this necessary consideration for individuals and minority groups is the search for a compromise akin to the concept of '*reasonable accommodation*'. Moreover, it is pleasing that the concept of reasonable accommodation also appeals to reason in order to evaluate the acceptability of accommodations. If one adheres to the ratio between reason and justice, these accommodations cannot go so far as to creating injustices, but on the contrary aim at avoiding them by ensuring equity. The Court gives as an example the institution of the civil service, which allows respecting the minority beliefs of objectors without creating inequality between conscripts.

ii *Obligations of Public Authorities in Case of an Objection Based on a Religious Belief*

α Reconciling the Rights instead of Opposing Them

Public authorities should therefore be enlightened by a whole set of values—human dignity, pluralism, tolerance and compromise—concerning the attitude which they are to adopt toward a conscientious objector who invokes a religious belief against the execution of an order. They must act in the light of these values while assuming their responsibility to ensure the common good

235 ECHR, *Leyla Şahin v. Turkey*, § 108.

236 *Idem.*

of society. Having regard to these values, how necessary is it to coerce or sanction the conscientious objector?

When two rights of equal value oppose each other in a given situation, public authorities should generally seek a balance between these rights, which leads, in practice, to the prevalence of one over the other depending on the circumstances. But as far as conscientious objection is concerned, another approach should be adopted, since it is impossible to limit or cut down on negative freedom of conscience (not being compelled to act against one's beliefs) without, at the same time, setting it at naught. Consequently, the State is obliged to *reconcile* competing rights so that they can coexist and so that both can be entirely respected. The responsibility to find a way of reconciling those rights rests on the State.

Such an approach goes beyond the requirements of strict commutative justice in so far as its aim is that everyone can enjoy concrete and effective rights.[237] The said approach, more distributive, is based on the principle of equality according to which a person or a group, for the sole reason that it is a minority, should not be subjected to unequal treatment in the effective enjoyment of human rights. The corollary of this approach is the principle of non-discrimination. The State must take measures to preserve minorities so that they are not indirectly discriminated against by the choices of the majority. Thus, when the ECtHR judges that the State has the positive obligation to respect a right, *"The verb 'respect' means more than 'acknowledge' or 'take into account'. In addition to a primarily negative undertaking, it implies some positive obligation on the part of the State."*[238] This is a way for society to self-limit its collective hold on individuals and to remain liberal.

As concerns alimentary rules of a religious nature, the ECtHR established the existence of a positive obligation for the State to offer food compatible with the religion of detained persons.[239] Not only can the State not compel *de facto* a prisoner to consume food contrary to his religious beliefs, but as much as possible, it must make provisions for the prisoner to eat without his religion being a source of inequality of treatment for him. In addition, the State cannot compel an adult endowed with reason to undergo a blood transfusion when the corresponding refusal is dictated by a religious belief, even *"regardless of how irrational, unwise or imprudent such choices may appear to others"*.[240]

237 ECHR, *Artico v. Italy*, n° 6694/74, 13 May 1980, § 33.

238 ECHR, *Folgerø and others v. Norway*, § 84.

239 ECHR, *Vartic v. Romania* (n° 2), n° 14150/08, 17 December 2013.

240 ECHR, *Jehovah's Witnesses of Moscow v. Russia*, n° 302/02, 10 June 2010, § 136.

Concerning military service, the ECtHR considered, in its judgment in the *Bayatyan* case, that respect for objectors' freedom of religion and conscience implies a positive obligation on the State to organise the operation of this service so that objectors' rights are respected, which is to say that the State is bound to propose an alternative to armed service. According to the Court, it is the absence of alternative which establishes the disproportionate character of the inflicted punishment. An action by the State which aims at reconciling its own rights with those of the objectors, rather than having them prevail over the latter, can *"ensure cohesive and stable pluralism and promote religious harmony and tolerance in society."* (§ 126)

On this same question of military service, the Human Rights Committee noted, in support of recognition of the right to conscientious objection, *"that respect on the part of the State for conscientious beliefs and manifestations thereof is itself an important factor in ensuring cohesive and stable pluralism in society"*[241] and that it is *"possible, and in practice common, to conceive alternatives to compulsory military service"*.[242] The bodies of the United Nations have specified what should be the qualities of such alternatives: service possibly imposed in substitution for military service must be compatible with the motives of conscientious objection and it must not be equivalent to a punishment;[243] and it should *"be a real service to the community and compatible with respect for human rights"*.[244] *Mutatis mutandis*, these characteristics can be required for any alternative service to any legitimate objection.

More generally, and as observed by Judges Tulkens, Popovic and Keller in a case regarding the refusal of a jurisdiction to adjourn a hearing scheduled for a Shabbat day, this positive obligation of the State consists in implementing *"reasonable accommodations"*, even if it means granting *"a few concessions"*, because it is also *"the small price to be paid in order to ensure respect for freedom of religion in a multicultural society"*.[245] Recently, the PACE adopted this approach based on the concept of reasonable accommodations.[246]

It should be remembered, however, that in contrast to "moral objections", which are based on justice, religious objections can be sanctioned, and even

---

241 HRC, *Yeo-Bum Yoon and Mr Myung-Jin Choi v. Republic of Korea*, § 84.

242 *Idem.*

243 Commission of Human Rights, Resolution 1998/77, OP4; HRC, *Yeo-Bum Yoon and Myung-Jin Choi v. Republic of Korea.*

244 HRC, *Cenk Atasoy and Arda Sarkut v. Turkey*2012, § 10.4; HRC, *Jeong and others v. Republic of Korea*, 24 March 2011.

245 ECHR, *Sessa v. Italy*, joint dissenting opinion, § 13.

246 PACE, Resolution 1846 (2011) *Combating all forms of discrimination based on religion*, and Resolution 2036 (2015), *Tackling intolerance and discrimination in Europe with a special focus on Christians.*

coerced in exceptional cases, if it proves necessary in a "*democratic society*" in view of its fundamental values.

ß The Basic Values of Society as a Limit

Though the practice of reasonable accommodation may give rise to criticism because of its intrinsic relativism and the inconvenience it causes in society, the needful setting of limits to tolerance is however delicate, since it necessarily implies affecting pluralism and partly giving up relativism. Indeed, tolerance and pluralism oppose that social cohesion and unity which public authorities may wish to maintain.

The ECtHR is not insensitive to such arguments. Thus, it is by fear of religious intolerance and communitarianism that the Court refrained from granting real scope to the educative rights of parents. In cases concerning a Christian family's refusal to submit to the general prohibition of home education by Germany,[247] and to the compulsory nature of sexual education lessons given in schools, the Court judged that these obligations are *"in line with the Court's own case-law on the importance of pluralism for democracy"* and that the school is *"aimed at educating responsible and emancipated citizens capable of participating in the democratic processes of a pluralistic society with a view, in particular, to integrating minorities and avoiding the formation of religiously or ideologically motivated "parallel societies."*[248] The Court even underlined that *"Sexual education should encourage tolerance between human beings irrespective of their sexual orientation and identity."* This decision should therefore be read more like the condemnation of a religious minority, perceived as intolerant in the name of tolerance and pluralism promoted by the authorities, rather than a compromise between competing rights, since the granting of an exemption from the sexual education lesson would represent only a meagre concession. It would not cause any harm to third persons and would allow respect for parents' educative rights in moral matters.

The position according to which a conscientious objector cannot effectively claim, in the name of tolerance, respect for opinions perceived as intolerant by the authorities was expressed also by the ECtHR in *Eweida and others v. United Kingdom*, already mentioned in this study. This case concerned, among others, the dismissal of a municipal employee (Mrs Ladele) caused by her religious opposition to the registration of civil unions between persons of the same sex. The Court validated this dismissal precisely in the name of the policy of *"equality and non-discrimination"* applied by the employer of this person.

---

247 ECHR, *Konrad and others v. Germany*, dec., n° 35504/03, 11 September 2006.

248 ECHR, *Dojan and others v. Germany*.

As to the wearing of the full-face veil,[249] the ECtHR accepted its prohibition in the name of the requirements related to the rights of others and the value of an open democratic society.

Ultimately, these examples illustrate the impossibility of forming a perfectly tolerant and pluralistic society, since such a society—supposing it may be formed—would have to give up every substantial value. The attempt at liberalisation and axiological neutralisation of democracy by the reorganisation of the latter through non-substantial instrumental values does not seem to have succeeded in liberating society from a certain moralism, because these instrumental values (such as pluralism, tolerance and non-discrimination, or abstract freedom and equality) have become values *per se*. Thus, although public morality changes, it does not disappear; the reverse is the case. It even seems to increasingly invest the legal field, which is now brought to govern matters that formerly escaped its area of competence.

The same examples also illustrate the fact that reasonable accommodation is possible only between relative values, i.e. values available and exchangeable on the values market of a pluralistic society, but that they cannot be conceded at the expense of values which structure and circumscribe pluralistic society itself. In this connection, the Parliamentary Assembly of the Council of Europe, in its Resolution n° 2076 of 30th of September 2015 on the *"freedom of religion and living together in a democratic society"*, affirmed that *"the shared values and principles which underpin 'living together' in our democratic societies* [...] *are non-negotiable"* and that they *"consist mainly of profound respect for human dignity and the fundamental rights* [recognised in Europe] *as well as respect for democratic principles and the rule of law, including the principle of non-discrimination between the different groups which make up our plural societies"*.

Nevertheless, the assertion of the supremacy of human rights over religions is relevant only insofar as the latter are anchored in justice and do not become an ideology, that is, a mere instrument of power or an alternative religion. In view of this, it is necessary to maintain a clear vision of morality as a rational way—distinct from religions, ideologies and individual subjectivism—to determine what is good or just in a given situation.

Conscientious objection is not just an aspect of freedom of conscience; it is also a warning for the whole society. If many people refuse to perform an act, public authorities should not try to force them to perform that act, but should question the reasons for this refusal, because it is not the law, but the personal conscience that is the ultimate witness of justice.

249 ECHR, *S. A. S. v. France*, GC, n° 43835/11, 1 July 2014.

Table of Authorities

Human Rights Committee

European Court of Human Rights

European Commission of Human Rights

European Committee of Social Rights

Committee of Ministers of the Council of Europe

Recommendation R(87)8 of 9 April 1987 regarding conscientious objection to compulsory military service.
Recommendation CM/Rec(2010)4 of 24 February 2010 on the human rights of the members of the armed forces.

Parliamentary Assembly of the Council of Europe

Resolution 337 (1967) on the right of conscientious objection.

Recommendation 1518 (2001) of the 1 March 2002, on the exercise of the right of conscientious objection to military service in Council of Europe member states.

Resolution 1728 (2010), Discrimination on the basis of sexual orientation and gender identity.

Resolution 1763 (2010), The right to conscientious objection in lawful medical care.

Resolution 1846 (2011), Combating all forms of discrimination based on religion.

Resolution 1928 (2013), Safeguarding human rights in relation to religion and belief, and protecting religious communities from violence.

Resolution 2036 (2015), Tackling intolerance and discrimination in Europe with a special focus on Christians.

Bibliography

Monographs and Chapters

Beausse de la Hougue, Claire de, *La liberté religieuse en Europe*, ANRT, 2005.

Bielefedt, Heiner, Ghanea, Nazila, Wiener, Michael, *Freedom of Religion or Belief, An International Law Commentary*, Oxford University Press, 2016.

Doe, Norman, *Law and Religion in Europe: A Comparative Introduction*, Oxford University Press, 2011.

Ferrari, Silvio, *Routledge Handbook of Law and Religion*, Routledge, 2015.

Ferrari, Silvio, Sabrina Pastorelli, *Religion in Public Spaces: A European Perspective*, Routledge, 2016.

International Theological Commission, *In Search of a Universal Ethics: A New Look at the Natural Law*, Rome, 2009.

Knittel, François, *Préceptes affirmatifs et préceptes négatifs chez saint Thomas d'Aquin*, Clovis, 2012.

Navarro-Valls, Rafael, Martínez-Torrón, Javier, *Conflictos entre conciencia y ley. Las objeciones de conciencia*, Iustel, 2011.

Perrenx, Jean-Pascal, *Théologie morale fondamentale. Tome 3: La conscience*, Téqui, 2008.

Puppinck, Grégor, *Droit et prévention de l'avortement en Europe*, Les Études Hospitalières, 2016.

Suaudeau, Jacques, *L'objection de conscience ou le devoir de désobéir : Ses origines et son application dans le domaine de la santé*, Peuple libre, 2013.

Takemura, Hitomi, *International Human Right to Conscientious Objection to Military Service and Individual Duties to Disobey Manifestly Illegal Orders*, Springer, 2009.

Temperman, Jeroen, *State-Religion Relationships and Human Rights Law: Towards a Right to Religiously Neutral Governance*, Brill, 2010.
Vickers, Lucy, *Religious Freedom, Religious Discrimination and the Workplace*, Bloomsbury Publishing, 2008.

Articles

Cranmer, Frank, "Conscientious objection to military service again: Enver Aydemir v Turkey", *Law & Religion UK*, 2016.
Martínez-Torrón, Javier, "Limitations on religious freedom in the case law of the European Court of Human Rights", *Emory Int'l L. Rev.*, Vol. 19, 2005.
Perry, Michael J., "Human Rights Theory, 4: Democracy Limited: The Human Right to Religious and Moral Freedom", *Emory Legal Studies Research Paper* No. 15-355, 2015.
Sawicki, Nadia N., "Doctors, Discipline, and the Death Penalty: Professional Implications of Safe Harbor", *Yale Law & Policy Review*, Fall, 2008.

www.ingramcontent.com/pod-product-compliance
Lightning Source LLC
Chambersburg PA
CBHW031333230926
51848CB00001B/211
9789004341593